ASTROLOGICAL PREDICTIONS

ASTROLOGICAL PREDICTIONS
A Revolutionary New Technique

R. Roy Whitney

International Standard Book Number 0-917086-56-2

Cover Design by Lou Geanoulis

Printed in the United States of America.

Published by ACS Publications, Inc.
P.O. Box 16430
San Diego, CA 92116

Dedicated
to
DESTNNE —
until the edge of time —
Roy

Also by ACS Publications

The American Atlas
The American Book of Tables
The American Ephemeris for the 20th Century [Midnight]
The American Ephemeris for the 20th Century [Noon]
The American Ephemeris for the 21st Century
The American Ephemeris 1901 to 1930
The American Epehmeris 1931 to 1940
The American Ephemeris 1931 to 1980 & Book of Tables
The American Ephemeris 1941 to 1950
The American Ephemeris 1951 to 1960
The American Ephemeris 1961 to 1970
The American Ephemeris 1971 to 1980
The American Ephemeris 1981 to 1990
The American Ephemeris 1991 to 2000
The American Sidereal Ephemeris 1976 to 2000
The American Heliocentric Ephemeris 1901 to 2000
The Asteroid Ephemeris: Dudu, Dembowska, Pittsburgh & Frigga
    (Stark & Pottenger)
The American Book of Nutrition and Medical Astrology (Nauman)
Basic Astrology: A Guide for Teachers and Students (Negus)
Basic Astrology: A Workbook for Students (Negus)
The Cosmic Clocks (Gauquelin)
Cosmic Combinations (Negus)
Expanding Astrology's Universe (Dobyns)
Healing With the Horoscope (Pottenger)
Interpreting the Eclipses (Jansky)
The American Book of Charts (Rodden)
The Gauquelin Book of American Charts (Gauquelin)
Astrological Insights Into Personality (Lundsted)
The Fortunes of Astrology (Granite)
Planetary Planting (Riotte)
Planting by the Moon 83/84 (Best & Kollerstrom)
Small Ecstasies (Owens)
The Only Way to. . . Learn Astrology, Vol. I
    Basic Principles (March & McEvers)
The Only Way to. . . Learn Astrology, Vol. II
    Math & Interpretation Techniques (March & McEvers)
The Only Way to. . . Learn Astrology, Vol. III
    Horoscope Analysis (March & McEvers)
The Lively Circle (Koval)
The Psychology of the Planets (F. Gauquelin)
Tomorrow Knocks (Brunton)
The Body Says Yes (Kapel)

TABLE OF CONTENTS

ILLUSTRATIONS

Figure   **Page**

ACKNOWLEDGMENTS

I wish to express heartfelt thanks to the people who have helped me with this book in its several stages. There are the people who gave me feedback when I orally and with brief papers presented some of the ideas and results that are presented in this book. The enthusiasm of their responses helped support me when I undertook the expansion of my research and the writing. When the book was in its draft form, several people read it, giving me gratefully received feedback. Maritha Pottenger, editor at ACS, both provided feedback and took the book through the editorial processes.

Three of the people who supported this work are specifically mentioned in this book. Neil F. Michelsen of ACS encouraged me to get my results in book form. He is publishing this book and is making this system of astrology available as one of ACS's offerings. Michael Erlewine of Matrix Software gave me encouragement to pursue this project and is developing related software for use on home computers. My friend, Larry Ely, has for years encouraged and helped me with some of the detailed research, planetary computer algorithms and related discussions that I have used as one of the cornerstones of this book.

My heartfelt thanks goes out to all of these people.

PREFACE

This work represents what I see as a preliminary exploration of a technique for assessing planetary keys to future trends among individuals, institutions and nations. This procedure has not been subjected to broad scrutiny by knowledgeable researchers in the astrological field.

However, because of the striking results presented in graphic form at the 1982 AFA Convention in Chicago, I thought that Dr. Whitney's work deserved broad circulation, assuming he was ready to do further investigation and put his material in a format suitable for publication as a book.

That he has fulfilled his part of the bargain is evidenced by the book that is in your hands. I encourage every reader to put the techniques outlined by Dr. Whitney to the test.

Unfortunately, the calculations are so complex that they can only be accomplished by a computer. Therefore, to use this approach, you have several options:

1) You can order the Dynamic Astrological Report from Astro Computing Services.

2) Order the program to do this calculation from Matrix Software or Astro-Graphics Services.

3) Program the calculations yourself on your own computer using the algorithms (step-by-step procedures to transform a given input to a given output) published in this book.

I have printed a smaller quantity of this book than usual because I expect your feedback and further work by Dr. Whitney to require substantial enhancement, if not fundamental change, of the material presented here. It will be easier to publish the follow-up book if the first edition is completely sold out!

One of the characteristics of the work of researchers done in other fields is the reporting in professional journals of the efforts to replicate the results of the pioneering researcher. Astrology is beginning to have journals appropriate for the publication of the more scholarly and scientific research efforts of astrologers. The British journal *Correlation* is one such journal. Other publications include *Astro-Psychological Problems: A Quarterly Research Journal*; *KOSMOS* (Journal of the International Society of Astrological Research); *Geocosmic Research Monographs* published by the National Council for Geocosmic Research; and *The Mutable Dilemma*. No revised edition or follow-up to this book will be considered until after there is broad-based discussion, communication, replication and argument about the validity of the approaches described in this book.

— Neil F. Michelsen

INTRODUCTION AND KEY TERMS

This book is unique. There is no other astrology text like it. In the forthcoming chapters, over two hundred years of historical events and personages will be astrologically analyzed with detail and clarity using graphs. The timing of major changes is readily apparent in these dramatic graphs. Plus, several explicit predictions are given for economic and political institutions in the world during the decade of the 1980s.

All of this has been made possible by the development of a new computer-based astrological tool called **Dynamic Astrology**. A discussion of the creation of Dynamic Astrology along with the basic concepts is given in the first chapter. Recognizing that many readers of this book will not have had astrological training, the astrological details have been placed in the appendices.

The scope of the results and the implications may be surprising to the reader not familiar with astrology. For some, the results may help clarify the reasons humanity has studied astrology during all known history. Astrology is one of the keys to human nature and activities, especially to cycles and the timing of people's lives. Tools as powerful as Dynamic Astrology may not always have been available, but persistence and talent can make up for many things — and some of the ancient astrologers had both.

To the astrologically trained reader, note that while Dynamic Astrology takes a quantum step beyond conventional astrology, it is consistent with conventional astrology. Dynamic Astrology gives decades of an entity's life or a group of entities' lives in two graphs. The key times of greatest change are seen in a moment. Then more conventional analyses are applied to observe the character of the related events. Dynamic Astrology also indicates each entity's major focus among the various planetary themes. A fascinating, new way of studying natal information is discussed in Appendix A.

The first chapter gives the central concept of interpretation for the graphs and a discussion of the meaning of "Intensity of Changes" and -I- and -S-values. The abbreviations used for several of the nations and world organizations are listed below. To help the reader who is not trained in astrology, some key terms and planetary key words are also listed below.

Abbreviations

ABG	Atomic Bomb Group
EEC	European Economic Community, also known as the Common Market
IMF	International Monetary Fund
OPEC	Organization of Petroleum Exporting Countries
PRC	People's Republic of China
UN	United Nations
USSR	Union of Soviet Socialist Republics
US	United States of America

Key Terms

Aspect
The angle formed between any two planets in the plane of the ecliptic where the Earth is at the center of the system. The two planets may in general be natal, progressed, transiting (defined below) or combinations thereof. Certain aspects have standard names. A few of them and their angles in degrees are:

Conjunction	0
Sextile	60
Square	90
Trine	120
Opposition	180

Natal Chart
The position of the planets in the plane of the ecliptic relative to the Earth at the time of birth of an entity. This is also known as the natal horoscope.

Orb
Any two planets seldom form any particular aspect exactly. The orb is a measure of leeway — the variance we allow. Orb measures how many degrees away from the exact aspect the planets may be, while still considering the aspect to be existent.

Plane of the Ecliptic
The plane formed by the Earth's revolution around the Sun.

Progressions
Solar progressions are used in this book. Solar progressions are almost the same as secondary progressions. (An article by Larry Ely in *MATRIX* Magazine, No. 9, 1982, explains the usually small but important

differences. See the Matrix Software ordering form at the end of this book for the address of Matrix publications.) With solar progressions a horoscope is created for the number of days after the birth date which are equal to the age of the entity in years. For example, if you are forty years old, a horoscope is calculated for forty days after your birthday. The horoscope is assumed to symbolize the patterns of your fortieth year. The aspects in the progressed chart and the aspects formed between the natal chart and progressed chart are considered in the calculations.

Transits   The positions of the planets in the plane of the ecliptic for any given moment in time are called transits or transiting planets. The aspects formed between the transiting planets and the planets in the natal chart are called the transiting aspects or transits. In this work, transits shall refer specifically to aspects between natal (birth) positions and transiting positions of the planets.

Planetary Key Words*

Planet**	Key Words
Sun	Leader, Self, Will, Self Esteem, Pride
Moon	Public, Subconscious, Home, Family
Mercury	Communications, Reason
Venus	Sensuality, Possessions, Pleasures, Science***
Mars	Physical Devotion, Self Expression, Military
Jupiter	Personal Growth, Belief Systems, Trust, Goals
Saturn	Identity and Responsibility in Space and Time, Realism, Practicality, Science
Uranus	"Higher" Mind, Electricity, Originality, Independence
Neptune	Idealism, Devotion, Deception, Oil and Biochemicals
Pluto	Organization, Will, Transformation

*   Love is a key word for all of the planets. No one planet has love exclusively to itself although certain ones work with it more extensively.
**   The Sun and Moon are not planets, but for simplicity of expression, whenever the word planet(s) is used, the Sun and Moon are included.
*** Venus's impact on individuals is so strong in the areas of their lives which are indicated by the first three key words, that its connection to science is usually missed. See Alice Bailey's material on the Venus/Earth connection, the Ray assignment of Venus and its mental characteristics.

CHAPTER I

DYNAMIC ASTROLOGY'S DEVELOPMENT

In the process of studying and practicing astrology, I found several features of astrology in need of development. The features can be stated as questions: how do I get my results into symbols or a language that a nonastrologer can comprehend? Many more people would use astrology if its information were also presented using modern symbols such as graphs. For that reason this book, with the exception of the appendices, assumes an intelligent but not necessarily astrologically trained reader.

Next came questions of weighting and scale. For example, is a Venus square Mars aspect more of a challenge than a Mercury opposition to Saturn? And, what if Neptune is or is not trine the Moon at the same time? The question of scale extends over time. How does the scale of astrological activity at one point in time compare to another point five, ten or even a hundred years later? Or, for that matter, is an astrological chart for an entity such as a country even valid after a hundred years, as the textbooks claim?

A most unsatisfying feature of astrology for me was the treatment of progressions as compared to transits. Some astrological texts touted progressions, some transits, some both. In my personal investigations I have found both worked, but not in a consistent manner. I found the usual simplistic concept of progressions being an inner psychological pattern that was evolving in time while transits represented the influence of an entity's external environment appeared to have some validity. However, current concepts and techniques were insufficient for me. For all the things astrology could be used to do, it was still difficult to forecast the scale of astrological activity and, in particular, pick out for an entity those times when great changes would occur.

In the autumn of 1981, I began the evolution of Dynamic Astrology with a series of computer programs. I picked the charts of three individuals (one known publicly and two not so known) and one country to work with. My programs at that time would only go back to 1900. In my initial programs, I counted the transiting and progressed aspects in the charts. The first question that arose was: What orb should be used for the aspects? Fortunately, with a computer all one does is run the program with as many different orbs as one pleases and compare the outputs to get the answer to this question. At the same time I experimented with weighting the aspects. For example, oppositions were counted more than squares and, in turn, squares counted more than sextiles. Progress was made by a combination of trials, errors, successes and insights.

I discovered that neither the weighted sums of transits or progressions, nor the sum of the two, correlated adequately to the events, activities or changes in the entities' lives. Next, I took the step of adding additional weights to the aspects based on the specific planets involved, e.g., a Sun/Saturn conjunction was weighted more heavily than a Venus/Jupiter conjunction. (See Appendix B for a full discussion of the development of my weighting system.) The results were still disappointing.

It was at this point that I had the insight to try multiplying the weighted sums of the transits times the weighted sums of the progressions. The results were immediately satisfying. The values calculated now strongly correlated with changes for the several entities' lives I was using for development work. I was ecstatic!

During the next several months I refined the weighting factors for the aspects and planets while investigating the graphs of several more entities. My first series of programs used only conjunctions and aspects that come from dividing 360 degrees by even numbers. I next created a program that used only conjunctions and aspects that come from 360 degrees divided by odd numbers. In early May I sent copies of some of my results to a few friends for evaluation and feedback.

The values calculated by the two programs related to the scale of changes in the entities' activities rather than to the level of activity. For this reason, the vertical graphs shown in the subsequent chapters are labeled **Intensity of Changes.** As an example of the difference between activity and change, international banking is always active, while going off the gold standard represented a major change. The values calculated by the program using the aspects formed with even numbers are labeled **-S- values.** Changes that correlate with high values of -S- tend to be stressful changes. The values calculated by the program using the aspects formed by the odd numbers are labeled **-I- values.** Changes that correlate with high values of -I- tend to be imaginative, creative, inspirational and cooperative changes. The examples in subsequent chapters help illustrate my use of these words.

I also evolved a central concept of interpretation as I studied the graphs of the values for various entities. Where both -I- and -S- are low, the existing conditions persist whether they are relatively active or inactive, happy or sad, etc. Changes are slow. With both -I- and -S- high, there are changing conditions under stress coupled with imaginative solutions to the challenges

involved. High -I- and low -S- implies change with ease. High -S- only implies stressful change. These interpretations are made in a framework where
ease and stress are relative terms. I also observed that doubling the value of
-I- or -S- corresponded to much more than a simple doubling in the amount
of changes experienced by an entity or group of entities. The more subtle
points of interpretations and use of the -I- and -S- values are presented in
the many examples in the subsequent chapters.

One of the areas of astrology that I have found most useful is the study
of compatibility between various entities, be they people, countries or events.
However, I again felt that there were unsatisfying features in the material as
typically presented, so I applied my new tool of Dynamic Astrology to groups
of entities early in my investigations. I quickly discovered that adding the
-I- or -S- of one entity to the -I- or -S- of another did not give clear results
correlating to relevant major events, while multiplying them did. Most of the
examples in the subsequent chapters involve groups of entities.

My goal to get astrological results in one of the modern symbol systems
has been achieved. The results can be conveniently expressed as a graph. Where
groups of entities are involved, each individual's -I- or -S- value is divided
by 700 at every point before the values are multiplied together to give the
resultant group value. The value of 700 was determined by the condition that,
independent of the number of entities forming the group, the maximum value
of the resultant group -I- or -S- values was usually in the range from 0.5 to 10.0.

I also discovered that Dynamic Astrology could be used to help with
the process of natal rectification. This important but very technical issue is
discussed in Appendix A, where all of the natal information is presented for
the examples used in this book.

Dynamic Astrology has also proved useful in determining which planets
in an entity's natal chart are most emphasized during a given event or change.
This is accomplished by calculating the -I- and/or -S- value for a given event
and then varying the strength of each natal planet to see which one produces
the greatest influence on the value. By using many events in an entity's life,
one can discover to which planet the entity is most attuned.

In August 1982 I had the pleasure of attending the convention of the
American Federation of Astrologers and the Astrological Conference on
Techniques in Chicago. I showed my work to several groups of people including Neil F. Michelsen of Astro Computing Services and Michael Erlewine
of Matrix software. Neil agreed to give me some computer codes to allow
me to calculate back before 1900. Now, Neil has published this book, implemented the Dynamic Astrology algorithms on his computer system and
offers Dynamic Astrology results as one of his many services. (See page 170.)
Michael is implementing the Dynamic Astrology algorithms as part of the
Matrix M-65 system of astrology programs for home and small business computers. Astro-Graphics Services also provides Dynamic Astrology for home
computers. (Information for ordering these programs is in the back of this
book.)

Dynamic Astrology is an evolving tool. It is an example of one of astrology's new directions as computers and new levels of awareness are integrated into the being of astrology. I hope you enjoy the examples I have included in this book, and wish you well in your applications of Dynamic Astrology.

CHAPTER II
UNITED STATES OF AMERICA

My first example of the use of Dynamic Astrology is the United States. Its history and main historical characters are quite well known, even outside the US, and a large variety of examples are available. In the chapter on World Powers, I return to the US where its relationship with several nations and events is considered.

Independence

The US was "born" on July 4, 1776, with the signing of the Declaration of Independence. I found with Dynamic Astrology that picking a very few people or entities as the keys to an event works quite well. To understand the timing of this event, I selected Benjamin Franklin — businessman, astrologer, colonial representative, scientist, postmaster, author and inventor; Thomas Jefferson — principal author of the Declaration of Independence; and George Washington — who was already the general of the American forces.

Figures II-1 and II-2 show the combined -I- and -S- values for these three individuals from 1770 to 1789. I use the combining method outlined in the Introduction and Chapter I. Throughout the book I used twenty-year time spans as a standard for the graphs. The following four events are indicated on these two figures:

A	7-4-1776	The Declaration of Independence is signed.
B	10-1777	British General John Burgoyne is defeated and the Convention of Saratoga occurs.
	2-1778	The Colonies form an alliance with France.
C	10-19-1781	British Lord Cornwallis surrenders, effectively ending the war.

D   9-17-1787   The US Constitution is completed and signed.

The combined -S- graph for Washington, Jefferson and Franklin shows its first high peak at the signing of the Declaration of Independence! (Figure II-2) The highest peak is six months later. These people were changing not only themselves but also their environment as they brought into existence a new entity, the United States of America. Though the changes were stressful and involved warfare, the result was a nation with significantly advanced concepts of freedom and the values of the human spirit. At the height of the Revolutionary War (event B), this group's combined -I- values show the second highest peak for the time period shown. These people were finding imaginative and cooperative solutions to very stressful challenges. The alliance with France was achieved in early 1778, and the war ran its course, effectively ending with the defeat and surrender of Lord Cornwallis (event C).

Frequently in the course of this book I will pick events and determine the most sensitive planet(s) in the relevant natal chart(s). This will acquaint the reader new to astrology with the themes of the planetary symbolism. On July 4, 1776, the most sensitive natal planet in George Washington's chart was Jupiter; in Thomas Jefferson's chart, Uranus; and in Benjamin Franklin's chart, Venus and the Sun were both active. The symbolism is accurate as Washington was the head of the Army, personally growing in stature and expanding the colonies' positions of strength. Jefferson was the intellectual giant and more. Franklin was the great universal man of the times, known for his sensuality, science, political and business skills, and the charming force of his personality.

In 1786 the highest -I- peak and a high -S- peak occur for the Franklin/ Jefferson/Washington group. These peaks correspond to the activities just before the calling of the Constitutional Convention in 1787. Great effort was required to unite the colonies and creatively formulate a viable new government. A high -S- peak is seen for the group at the completion of the Constitutional Convention. The stressful start of the Revolutionary War was followed by a stressful and inspirational, creative and cooperative formulation of a new form of government.

Before continuing with the US graphs, it is worth asking whether these three individuals could have had that much of an influence on the timing of events. Were these events just random events in the history of the world? Or were these events already timed and as these three individuals chose to take key parts in them, correspondingly had they chosen birth times to fit their parts in these events? My observations lead me to say both the first and last conclusions are in part correct. Our modern concept of randomness is just creativity and consciousness operating at the lowest or simplest levels of physical matter. Creativity is at every point and level a possibility. People can act at levels far beyond the random ones. These three individuals could have made other choices such that other people would have been the key people involved. The events, and possibly their timing, would have been

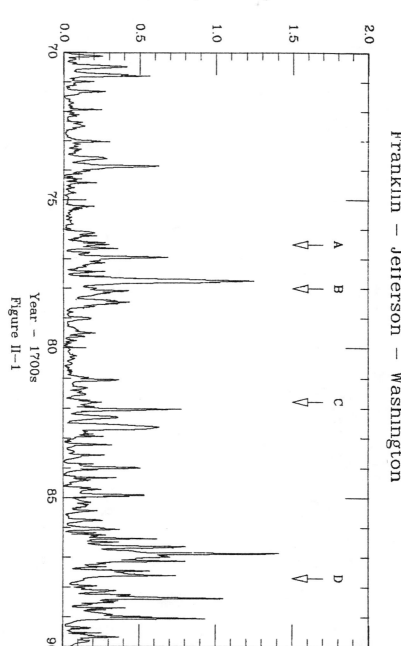

Franklin — Jefferson — Washington

Intensity of Changes
−I−

Year — 1700s

Figure II−1

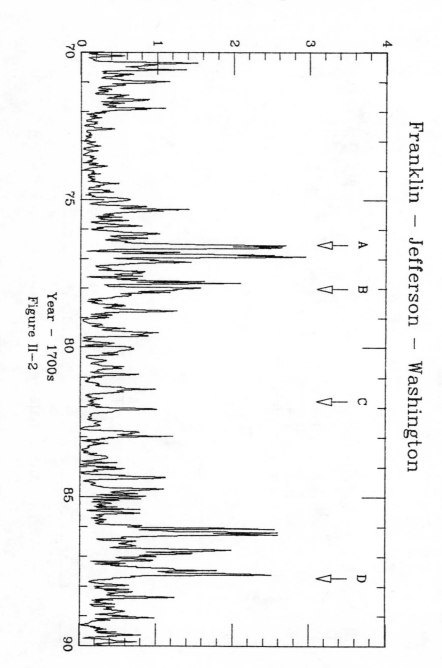

−S−
Intensity of Changes

Franklin — Jefferson — Washington

Year — 1700s
Figure II-2

different. The examples using Dynamic Astrology presented in this book will serve to support these observations.

Civil War

The Civil War was the most dramatic and emotional internal event in US history. Two differing political, social and economic systems struggled for control of the future of the country. At this point in time, the future was both symbolically and physically the western lands of America. The southern states were burdened by a poor economy and slavery. The northern states had the advantage of better technology and foreign trade. Both groups were burdened by poor social and military systems. If these systems had been better, they could have foreseen that war was the long-range result of their daily decisions and could have taken actions for alternative solutions.

Figure II-3 shows the Dynamic Astrology -S- values for the US during the period of the Civil War. Figure II-4 shows the graph for the combined -S- values of Abraham Lincoln and the US. There are four events indicated in these and the next several graphs:

E	3-6-1857	Dred Scott Decision of the Supreme Court.
F	Summer/ Fall 1858	Lincoln-Douglas Debates and election.
G	3-4-1861	Abraham Lincoln takes office of president.
	4-12-1861	Attack on Fort Sumter.
H	4-15-1865	Death of Abraham Lincoln.

Both graphs show their most pronounced peak in 1857 (event E) at the time of the Dred Scott Decision of the Supreme Court. With this decision the Court ruled that slavery, and thereby the southern states' political, social and economic system, could not be prohibited from spreading to all of the western territories. This future was unacceptable to the northern states. Their newly formed Republican political party rapidly gained support.

The next US election was in 1858. On the medium-high peak (labeled F) in the Abraham Lincoln–US graph of -S- values, Abraham Lincoln and Stephen Douglas debated the slavery issue across the state of Illinois. Lincoln lost the Illinois senatorial election but became known across the nation. In 1860 Lincoln won the presidency over Douglas and two other candidates. At the event labeled G in this set of graphs, Lincoln assumed the office of president and a month later the Civil War broke out.

The conditions that climaxed in the Civil War had been building for decades if not centuries. During the four-year period shown between events E and G in this set of graphs, the mainspring for the clock on the war was

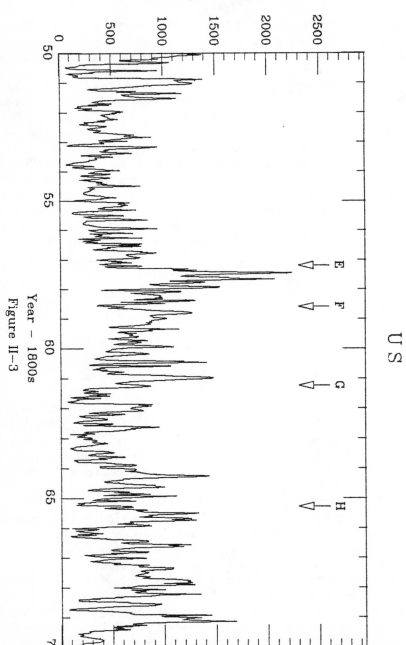

−S−
Intensity of Changes

U S

E
F
G
H

Year − 1800s
Figure II−3

-S-

Intensity of Changes

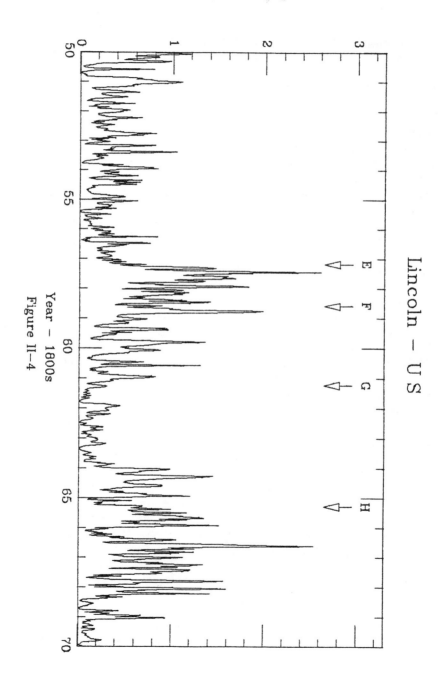

Lincoln – U S

Year – 1800s
Figure II-4

fully wound. The tension in the country is also indicated in the -S- values of the US Constitution graph (Figure II-5). The highest peak during this time period occurs in late 1859 as the groundwork was being laid by the southern states to break away from the northern states and form a separate government with its own constitution. The second highest peak occurs in 1856 as the Supreme Court took up the Dred Scott case.

The war was not going to be short, as people of the time had hoped. The mainspring was much too tightly wound. The first -S- peak after the start of the war in the Lincoln–US graph appears in early 1864 and this peak is not up to the size of those going into the war. After a medium level of intensity of change in this -S- graph for a year, the war did end. Shortly after, Lincoln was shot and died (event H).

The timing of the start of the US Civil War was also indicated by an astrological event contained in these Dynamic Astrology graphs though not explicitly shown by them. On April 14, 1861, the planet Neptune passed from the astrological sign of Pisces to the sign Aries. On April 12, 1861, the southern states' attack on Fort Sumter commenced. Neptune's energies feed into the passions of the masses or the public's subconscious. In Pisces the energies went into emotional and mystical passions. In Aries the Neptunian energies went into fiery impulsive activity. As an aside, note that when Neptune next went into a fire sign, Leo, the First World War had just begun; but when Neptune went into the subsequent fire sign, Sagittarius, the world did not see war so much as religious cults.

At the start of the Civil War the most sensitive planet in the US natal chart was Uranus. The most sensitive planets in Lincoln's natal chart on this date were Uranus, Saturn and the Moon. The Uranian emphasis in both Lincoln's and the US charts meant that the events taking place would have unexpected consequences and connections. The intelligence and electrical aspects of Uranian energies are also correct. The Civil War is usually considered the first modern war. The telegraph, the world's first useful electrical device, was used extensively in war communications for the first time and various technologies related to weaponry and transportation were exploited. Saturn denoted the consequences of past actions brought to home (the Moon) for the US. From the lessons learned, the country decided to go on without slavery.

It is also instructive to look at the -I- values in the Lincoln–US graph for the Civil War period (Figure II-6). The highest peaks are in the early 1850s, as Lincoln made plans for higher political offices, and the North-South conflicts were being resolved by less violent means. Except for one narrow medium high peak in late 1863, this -I- graph is very low during the period of two years before the war and during the war itself. Imaginative solutions to the challenges involving love, creativity and cooperation were not being formulated in such a way as to be listened to.

Franklin Delano Roosevelt

Franklin D. Roosevelt was elected to the US presidency on the highest -I- peak

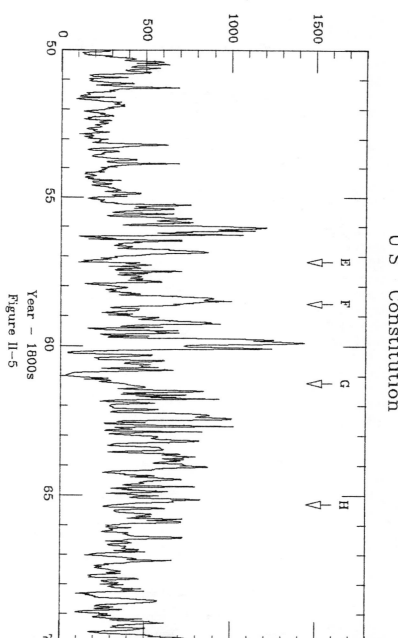

-S-
Intensity of Changes

US Constitution

Year – 1800s
Figure II-5

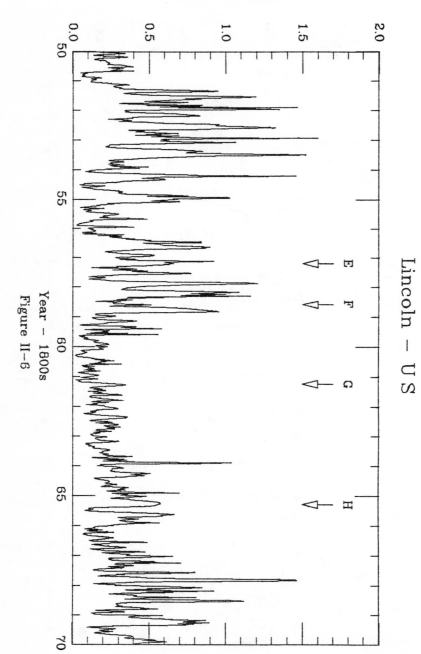

−I−
Intensity of Changes

Lincoln − U S

Year − 1800s
Figure II−6

shown in the combined Roosevelt–US graph (Figure II-7). His election was in the spirit of immediately getting the country out of the depression and onto the road of economic recovery. Roosevelt had a one-hundred-day honeymoon with Congress, where any legislation he desired was passed. Later analysis has shown that Roosevelt and the economists of the time did not know how to solve the economic challenges before them. The necessary computational tools required to adequately model the complex economic system were not available. The question of whether we have these tools available today is discussed in the chapter on World Banking. What Roosevelt did accomplish was the combined termination of some old policies and initiation of new programs. When coupled with the economic methods applied to run World War II, these programs did facilitate an economic recovery. Further, Roosevelt infused the country with a belief in itself that prepared it to meet the challenges of World War II and laid the foundation for a new generation of social legislation.

The events indicated in this set of figures are listed below:

I	11-8-1932	Election of Franklin D. Roosevelt
J	7-22-1937	Proposal to expand the Supreme Court defeated in the Senate
K	12-7-1941	Attack by Japan on Pearl Harbor bringing the US into World War II

Roosevelt's biggest political defeat in Congress came in response to his early 1937 proposal to expand the Supreme Court. At the second-highest -S- peak shown (event J) in the combined Roosevelt–US graph (Figure II-8), the Senate voted not to expand the court. Roosevelt's threat to the court was sufficient to have it no longer stop his programs, but the country was still in a general economic depression. As a separate issue, the country also went into a sharp recession that summer.

With the start of World War II on September 1, 1939, Roosevelt had to campaign for the 1940 election on the issue of keeping the country out of the war while subtly preparing the country for war. The Japanese attack on Pearl Harbor (event K in this set of graphs) came as a surprise to the average American but probably not to Roosevelt. The Roosevelt–US graph indicates this event with the highest -S- peak. During the course of the war, there was constant stressful change as shown in the Roosevelt–US graph. The end of the war in 1945 is marked by a short period of low stress and a medium-sized peak in the corresponding -I- graph. Roosevelt died just before the end of the war. The timing of World War II was not solely in the hands of the US. The next two chapters will show this.

The most sensitive planet in both Roosevelt's and the US natal charts

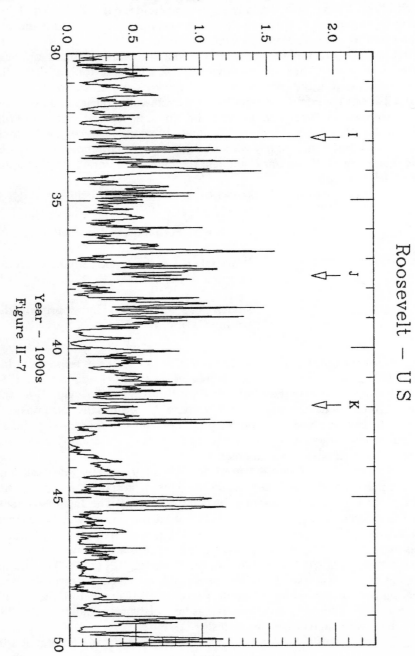

−I−
Intensity of Changes

Roosevelt − U S

Year − 1900s
Figure II−7

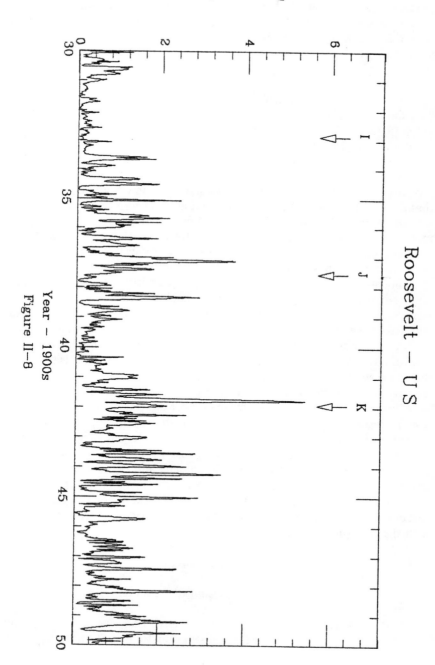

−S−
Intensity of Changes

Roosevelt − U S

Year − 1900s

Figure II−8

The most sensitive planet in both Roosevelt's and the US natal charts on the day of the Pearl Harbor attack was Pluto. Nuclear energy is associated with Pluto, and this war saw the development of nuclear weapons and their use to end the war. But Plutonian symbolism also relates to many other areas of human activity. This war saw the conscious, willful, orchestrated use of media, music, arts, technology, psychology and even astrology for political ends.

Richard Milhous Nixon

The single -S- spike in early 1972 in the Richard M. Nixon–US combined graph (Figure II-9) summarizes his presidency. In February 1972 Nixon opened the door to the People's Republic of China (PRC) with a dramatic personal visit. In May 1972 Nixon visited the Union of Soviet Socialist Republics, (USSR), and the Watergate break-in occurred in June 1972. In November 1972 Nixon was elected by the vote of every state but one. Many of the actions that effectively brought an end to the Vietnam War were also taken in 1972. On August 9, 1974, Nixon resigned the office of presidency to let the country move forward and to avoid facing a trial for impeachment.

The most sensitive planet in Nixon's natal chart at the time of the Watergate break-in was Neptune. He was deceitful and tried to sway public thinking and the media. He was more concerned with his image than his actions. Nixon had three equally sensitive natal planets at the time of his resignation: Saturn, Pluto and the Moon. Saturn indicates reaping the harvest of what has been sown. Pluto denotes the transformation of conditions, and the Moon is indicative of the change in his home as he left the White House. The Sun was the most sensitive planet in the US natal chart at this time. The Sun is the symbol of the self, and in a country's chart the leader of the country carries that symbol. The leadership of the US changed on that day.

Turning now to the -I- graph for the US for this time period (Figure II-10), it is interesting to note that while several medium peaks are observed, the highest peaks are in the time period between the Watergate break-in and Nixon's resignation. The changes the nation chose were to end the Vietnam War and not to tolerate the behavior of Nixon. The antiwar movements turned into environmental movements and the military licked its wounds.

Shown (Figures II-11 and II-12) are the -S- graphs for the US and the combination US–US Constitution for this time period. The peaks are labeled with the following events:

L	6-17-1972	Watergate Break-in.
M	8- 9-1974	Resignation of President Nixon.
N	9-27-1977	Thomas B. "Bert" Lance resigns as Office of Management and Budget Director.

−S−
Intensity of Changes

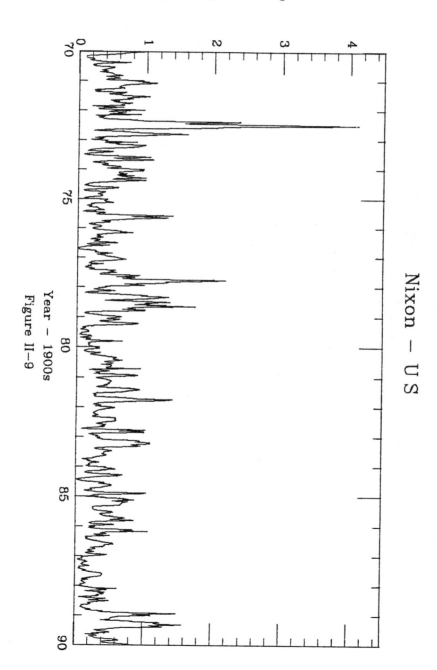

Nixon − U S

Year − 1900s

Figure II−9

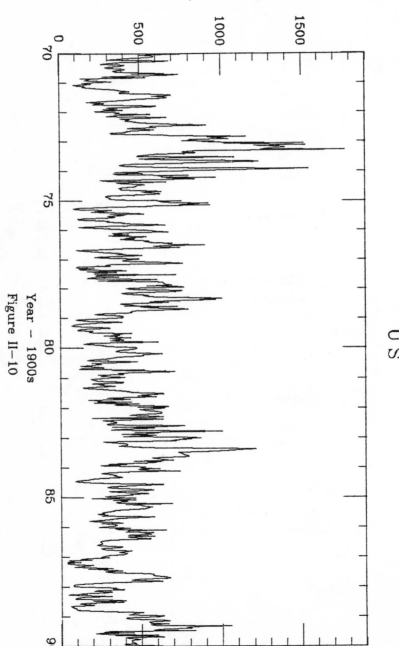

−I−

Intensity of Changes

U S

Year − 1900s

Figure II−10

O   9-17-1978   Camp David accords between Egypt and Israel.

                          Also at this time: Property tax limitations become law in California, the Equal Rights Amendment receives a controversial extension, and US foreign policy is in difficulties outside of Egypt and Israel as the Shah of Iran falls from power.

P   11-4-1980   Ronald Reagan is elected President and attempts to set the country right economically and with the USSR.

Q   9-2-1982   With expenditures of phenomenal amounts of money the Republicans hold their position in the US Senate but lose significant strength in the House and in state governorships. US unemployment reaches its highest mark since 1940. A new leader takes over in the USSR.

The highest -S- peak shown to date in this time period in the US–US Constitution graph has just occurred December 1982. The previous peaks have already been discussed or are adequately discussed in the event listing above. The astrological implication is that stressful changes are occurring that will significantly effect the US. Unemployment is at its highest level since the great depression of the 1930s, while in inflated current dollars, the stock market is at its highest level ever. The MX missile program does not have the support of Congress. There is new leadership in the USSR. A significant antinuclear movement has formed in both the US and western Europe. The United States allies, Great Britain and Argentina, have just finished a war. To top the list the projected 1983 budget deficit is $190 billion, not including state and local governmental amounts, and the world banking system is in trouble.

A Look Ahead

The current conditions in the US could be expected to continue until late 1988 or early 1989 (when the highest -S- peak occurs for this time period if judged only by the combined US–US Constitution graph). However, the highest -S- peak in the US graph occurs in 1986. The issues and related Dynamic Astrology graphs to be discussed in the chapter on the World Banking have not yet been considered. And, the graphs of the US president have not been included. Thus, conditions in the US may be expected to change sooner than 1989, but 1989 will most likely see the biggest changes.

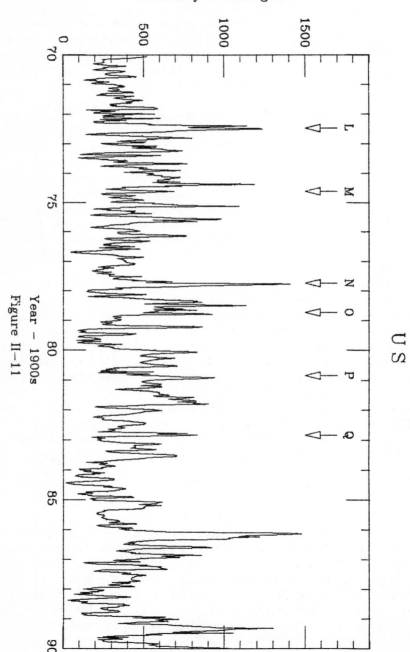

–S–
Intensity of Changes

Year – 1900s
Figure II–11

U S

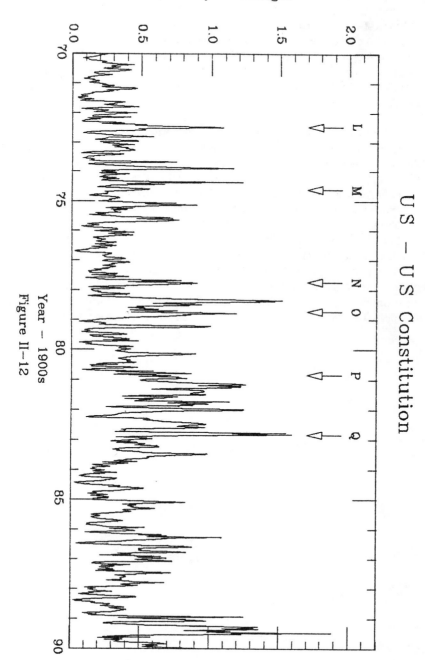

-S-
Intensity of Changes

US - US Constitution

Year — 1900s
Figure II-12

United States, Canada and Mexico

To conclude this chapter on the US, it is appropriate to include the Dynamic Astrology graphs combining the US graphs with those of its immediate neighbors, Canada and Mexico. Figures II-13 and II-14 give the US–Canada combined -I- and -S- graphs. We observe significant periods of high -I- values in the 1970s and early 1980s. The US and Canada have significantly increased trade in minerals, petroleum and other products during this time period. The long standing good relations between Canada and the US prevented the high -S- peak of 1978 from being an overly stressful period between the two countries. A high period of stress is yet to come and occurs in late 1988 and early 1989.

Before considering the present time period between the US and Mexico, it is interesting to consider their combined -S- graph for the period 1830-49 (Figure II-15). The high peak in late 1845 is just before the US–Mexican War which started in the spring of 1846 on April 15. The highest peak shown is shortly before the Treaty of Guadalupe Hidalgo. With that treaty, on February 2, 1848, the US acquired from Mexico the territories that are now the states of Arizona, California, Nevada, New Mexico, Utah and parts of Colorado.

The US–Mexico combined -I- and -S- graphs for the present are shown in Figures II-16 and II-17. The -I- peaks in the 1970s correspond in part to US investment in the Mexican oil fields. The largest -I- peak occurs in 1983. This will probably relate to events where the US will try to prop up the Mexican monetary system and economy. The combined-S- graph shows a single large peak in 1986. This peak is discussed in the chapter on World Powers.

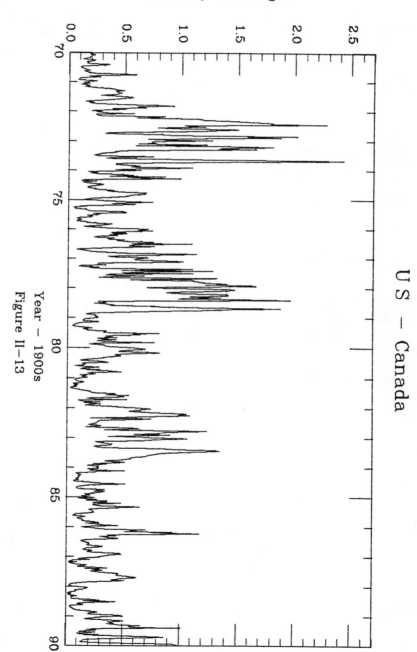

−I−
Intensity of Changes

U S − Canada

Year − 1900s
Figure II−13

-s-
Intensity of Changes

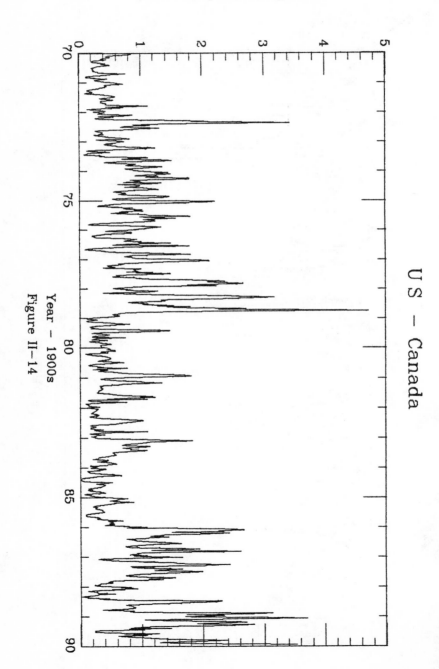

U S – Canada

Year – 1900s
Figure II–14

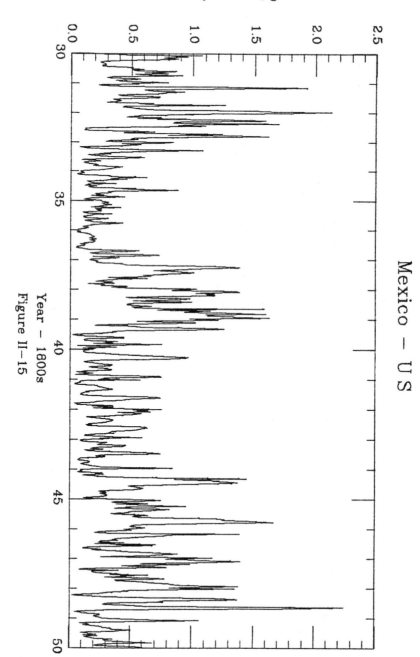

-S-
Intensity of Changes

Mexico – U S

Year – 1800s
Figure II–15

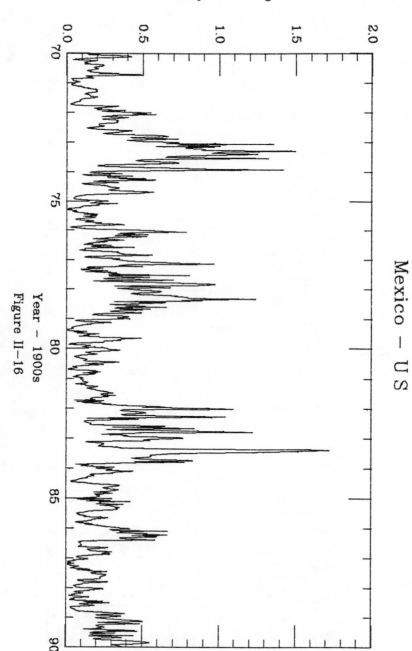

−I−
Intensity of Changes

Mexico − U S

Year − 1900s
Figure II−16

−S−
Intensity of Changes

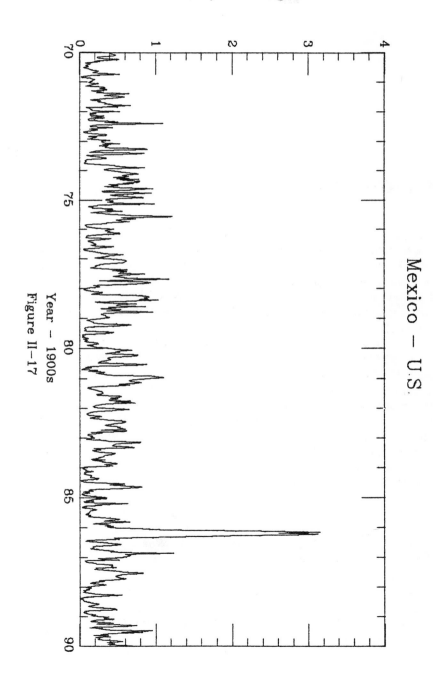

Mexico − U.S.

Year − 1900s
Figure II−17

CHAPTER III

GERMANY

Germany and Adolf Hitler make such an excellent example in astrology that the material has been overworked. At the same time, many astrologers do not like this material since they do not care to tune into Hitler. The material is being presented here because using Dynamic Astrology will shed some new light on the subject, examples in the previous and following chapters relate to the material, and many who read this book will not be aware of the existing analyses.

Three entities will make up the Germany Group. Two of the related "births" for these entities come from the formation of the united German state. On January 18, 1871, with the German armies surrounding Paris, Prussian Prince Otto von Bismarck's plans succeeded, and King William of Prussia was proclaimed emperor of a united Germany at the palace of Versailles. The second "birth" was when the first Reichstag of all Germany met and accepted the constitution on April 14, 1871. This act set up the unified government. Adolf Hitler is the third entity for the combined graphs of the German Group.

The -I- and -S- graphs for the German Group are shown in Figures III-1 and III-2 for 1910-29. The events labeled in these two figures are given below:

A	5-2-1913	Hitler arrives in Munich.
B	7-28-1914	Start of World War I.
	8-10-1914	Hitler enlists in the army.
C	10-5-1916	Hitler wounded in the leg.
D	2-24-1920	Hitler makes first speech.
E	11-8-1923	Beer Hall Putsch.

F   2-27-1925   Hitler resumes party leadership.

Hitler's arrival in Munich (event A) is a medium height -I- peak. The start of the war and his joining the army (event B) are both medium -I- and -S- peaks. His wounding (event C) is just after the largest -S- peak. It is at this time that Germany's position in World War I began to seriously deteriorate. Away from the front to recuperate, Hitler was aghast at the situation, the poor morale, and the lack of support for the war and its leaders. The year 1917 was difficult for Hitler, as he returned to new duties at the deteriorating front and for Germany as the US entered the war on April 6. The -S- value for the first half of 1917 is of medium height. On the next peak of the same height a year later, Hitler was gassed. A month later in November 1918, there was an armistice ending the war to which Hitler reacted violently. Note also that during the last year and a half of the war, the German Group's -I- value was particularly low. There was no mechanism, structure, or inspiration for a winning end or peaceful resolution of the war. There was only the waiting for the inevitable defeat. Though just one soldier among millions, Hitler's life had run in synchronization with the life of the German nation.

With event D (Hitler's first speech), Hitler began his rise as a public figure. The next several years show significant -I- strength as, with surprising ease, Hitler became a prominent public and political personage in the area of Germany around Munich. Germany itself began recovering from the war, but severe political and economic problems were present. The extremist parties, both left and right, gained the most popular support in mid-1920s. By the end of 1922, what cooperation there had been in the country's political system fell apart, although Hitler and his party had done quite well in bringing in people from the far right who had money and broader political connections.

At the height of the medium -S- peak in January 1923, French troops occupied the Ruhr. There was almost a state of war in the area. Inflation during the year was so high that it changed the mark from being almost worthless to worthless.

With several years of relatively easy successes behind them (event E), Hitler and his party tried to take over the government in Munich by force in their Beer Hall Putsch. The civil authorities stopped them. At the time of the Putsch, both the Group -I- and -S- values were low, although if you do Hitler's graphs, you will observe that they are briefly high. After the Putsch, conditions in the country remained in a state of economic disaster, but the political show calmed down. Germany was not ready for the changes that would occur with Hitler at the helm. He went off to jail for a year and wrote *Mein Kampf*. With his return to the political scene (event F), Hitler had a new plan and some significant -I- strength in the German Group to enable its implementation. Hitler, with calls to imagination, cooperation and initiative, would legally take the helm of Germany.

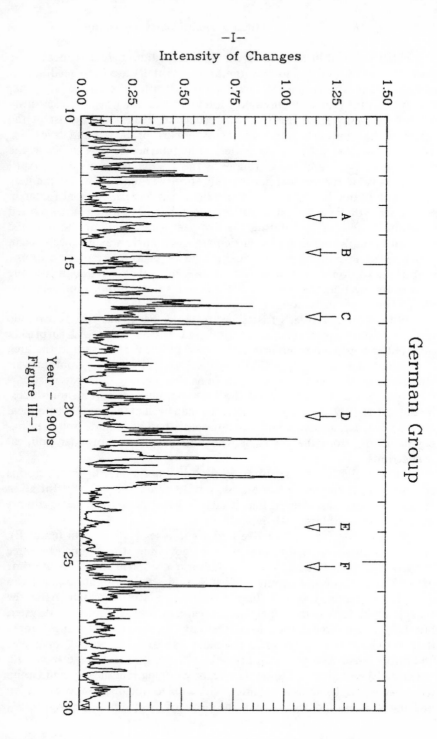

-I-
Intensity of Changes

German Group

Year - 1900s
Figure III-1

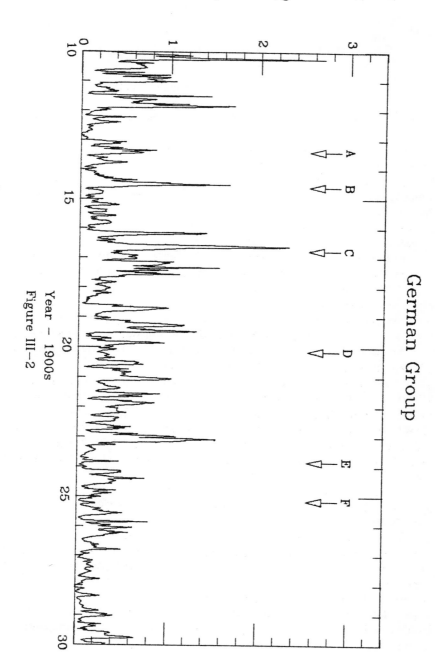

–S–
Intensity of Changes

German Group

Year – 1900s
Figure III–2

Focusing on the war years, consider now the -I- and -S- values for the next twenty years (Figures III-3 and III-4) for the German Group. The labeled events are listed below:

G	1-30-1933	Hitler becomes Chancellor of Germany.
H	9-01-1939	Germany invades Poland and World War II begins.
I	6-22-1941	Germany invades the USSR.
J	4-15-1945	Hitler dies and World War II ends in Europe.

From a year before Hitler became Chancellor (event G) until the start of World War II, the German Group shows significant -I- values and peaks. Hitler's plan had worked to bring him to power. He stayed with the plan to make changes in Germany, to keep himself in power and prepare for war. As for -S- strength, there is some around the time he became Chancellor, but very little within a few years afterwards. Hitler squelched opposition quickly and soon the Nazi party reigned supreme.

To use the image of a clock again, the German Group had wound up the mainspring of their war by mid-1939, as is indicated by the very large -I- peak that year. In September of that year, they started the war (event H). There was little inspiration for creative changes in their war plan once the war was underway. There is one sharp -S- peak in the first several years of the war in 1941. Six weeks after the peak, Germany invaded the USSR (event I).

At the start of the war in 1939, both of the natal charts for the birth of the unified Germany had two equally sensitive planets. Further, the two planets were the same for both charts: the Moon and Jupiter. Germany wanted growth (Jupiter) of their belief system to the point of world domination. The public's (Moon) feelings had been tuned to this desire by Hitler. The most sensitive planet in Hitler's natal chart on that day was the Sun with the Moon only slightly less sensitive. The Sun is the planet of the leader of the country. One of the ancient symbols of the solar force on the Earth was taken by the Nazis as their symbol, the swastika.

The -S- values begin to rise in mid-1944 when Germany was retreating on all fronts. During this time the German industries, large cities and military were destroyed while the V2 rockets hit London.

The Germans hoped for relief from the destruction of the war. The relief came via defeat. The date for this change in Germany is seen quite clearly in the German Group's -I- graph summer 1945. The Germans had the creative opportunity to begin rebuilding their country in the summer of 1945. As for the war, in August of 1945 the US exploded the nuclear bomb at Hiroshima, Japan. The US had the bomb, not Germany, and Hitler was dead in April by his own hand (event J). The clock on the war had run out for the German Group and did not get rewound.

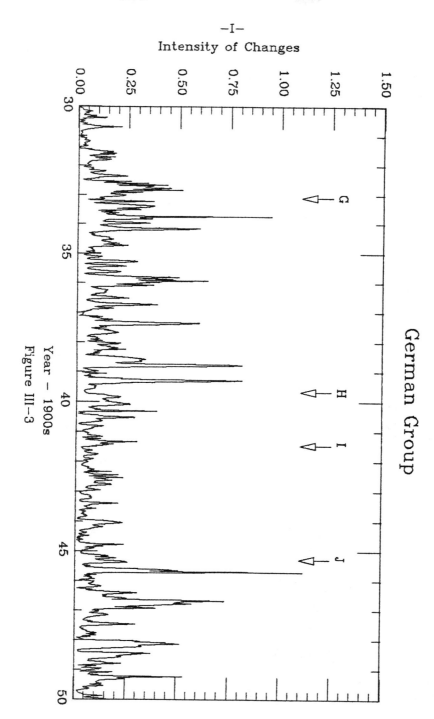

−I−
Intensity of Changes

German Group

Year − 1900s
Figure III−3

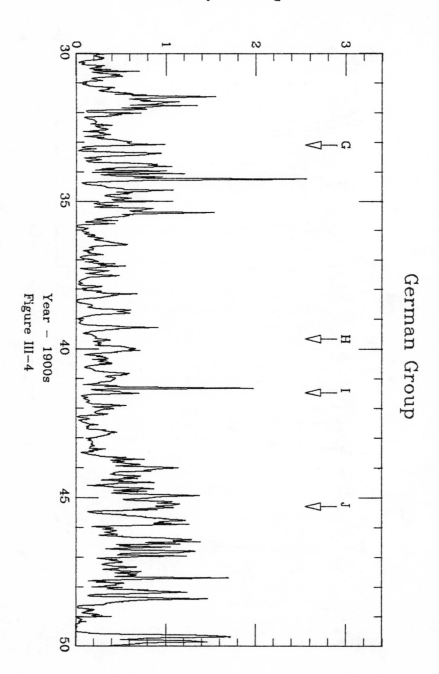

−S−
Intensity of Changes

German Group

Year − 1900s
Figure III−4

CHAPTER IV
RUSSIA, CHINA AND INDIA

Union of Soviet Socialist Republics

While Stalin was leader of his country, his highest -S- peak coincided with the German invasion of the USSR in the summer of 1941. Figure IV-1 shows the -S- values for Stalin from 1930-49. The combined -S- values for Stalin and the USSR are shown in Figure IV-2. The large peak in the late summer of 1940 corresponds to the taking of the Baltic Republics by the USSR and the preparations for the expanded war to come. The USSR -I- values for this time period are given in Figure IV-3 and the events labeled in these graphs are given below:

A	1929-30	Stalin takes power as dictator and begins the process of industrialization.
B	9-01-1939	German invasion of Poland.
	9-17-1939	USSR Invasion of Poland.
C	8-1940	Baltic Republics taken over and made republics in the USSR.
D	6-22-1941	German invasion of the USSR.
E	early 1949	Nationalist Chinese forces fall to Communist Chinese forces.

In early 1930 we observe both high -I- and -S- values as Stalin secured his positions of power. The high -I- value at this time implies that many of the changes that Stalin implemented were new, creative directions for the country. The high accompanying stress correlates with the bloody methods Stalin employed. In the 1936-38 period there were public trials of dissidents and

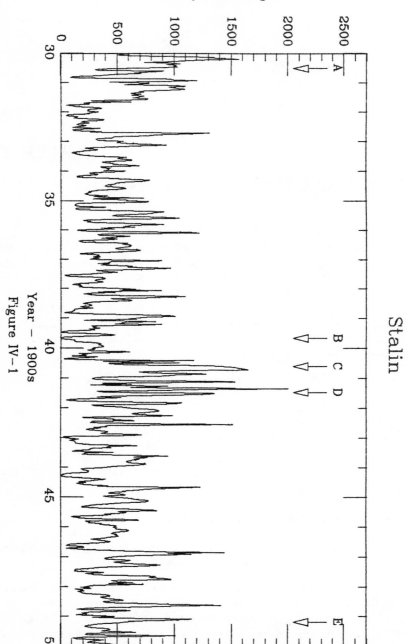

-S-
Intensity of Changes

Stalin

Year – 1900s
Figure IV-1

-S-
Intensity of Changes

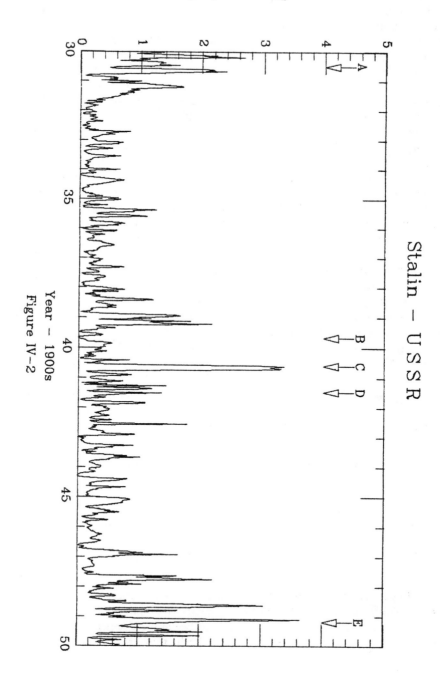

Stalin – USSR

Year – 1900s

Figure IV-2

several related purges. The -I- values for the USSR are very low and the -S-values are medium to low during this time.

For early 1939 there is a significant -S- peak in the USSR-Stalin graph. Hitler and Stalin were jockeying for positions as they prepared to take Poland in the autumn of 1939 (event B). The most sensitive planet in Stalin's natal chart at the time of the German invasion was Pluto, with Neptune and the Sun only slightly less sensitive. The willful (Plutonian) battle between the two leaders (Sun) focused the dreams and ideals (Neptune) of millions on their way to war. Also, Stalin felt deceived by Hitler, which is another characteristic sometimes associated with Neptune. Equally sensitive planets in the USSR's natal chart were the Sun and Moon. The people of the country are represented by the Moon and their leader the Sun (as discussed above). With the taking of the Baltic Republics and the German invasion, the war for the USSR was fully underway, with no relief until 1944 when the USSR -I- value begins to rise.

Following World War II, the USSR's relatively easy establishment of Communist governments in eastern Europe is seen by the very high -I- values for 1945-47 (Figure IV-3). However, the Chinese Communists taking power in China and establishing the People's Republic of China (PRC) was not such an easy birth for the USSR. The PRC established itself as an independent power not under USSR domination. Note that the birth of the PRC was not so stressful for Stalin as for the USSR. Stalin was soon to be gone; others would be dealing with the PRC.

It is interesting to note that the first nuclear reactor in the USSR began operating on December 25, 1946, the high point of the -I- values from 1930 to 1949. The first USSR nuclear bomb test was August 8, 1949. The high -S- point in the Stalin USSR graph is only a few months before this date. The USSR became a world nuclear power and the accompanying stressful responsibilities were acquired.

Skipping twenty years, we observe that the level of stress in the USSR has been relatively low in the period since 1970 (Figure IV-4). There are four events that match with the highest peaks for this time period:

F	2-18-1972	Richard Nixon's visit to the PRC.
G	10-16-1978	The election of the Polish Pope, John Paul II.
H	11-28-1979	The USSR invasion of Afghanistan.
I	11-12-1982	Andropov takes leadership.

Events G and H actually span one broad peak. The year 1984 shows a step up in -S- values for the USSR along with the highest peak during these two decades. There are also high peaks in early 1989. These peaks are discussed in the chapters on World Banking and World Powers.

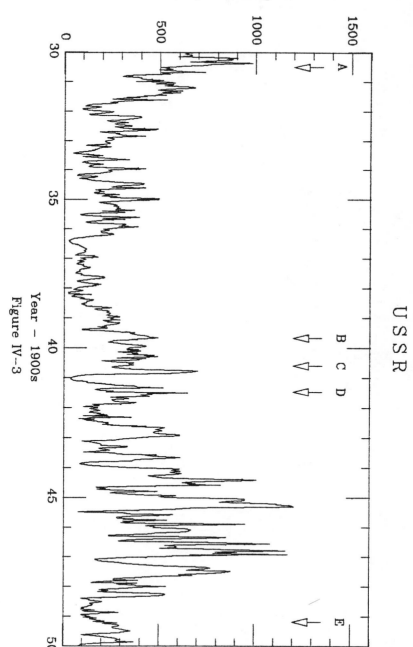

-I-
Intensity of Changes

USSR

Year — 1900s
Figure IV-3

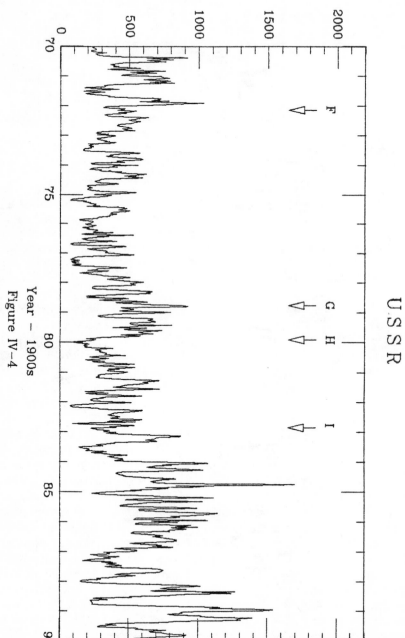

-S-

Intensity of Changes

USSR

Year — 1900s

Figure IV-4

People's Republic of China and India

Moving geographically slightly and backing up two decades, we will next consider the PRC and India. These two nations did not get along well during this time period, 1950-69. Their combined -S- graph is shown (Figure IV-5) and the labeled events are listed below:

J	6-10-1954	Chou En Lai and Nehru meet with a subsequent agreement between PRC and India.
K	8-1959	PRC moves troops into territory claimed by India.
L	10-11-1962	Border war between PRC and India.

In addition to the -S- peaks at events J and K, there is actually a higher peak one year later. This is an occasionally observed pattern in the graphs. When there are groups of closely spaced peaks of nearly the same heights, the slightly lower early peak may correspond to the related events.

Moving two decades forward, Figure IV-6 gives the most striking -I- peak to date for PRC and India as listed below:

M	4-15-1976	PRC and India announce the first exchange of ambassadors in fifteen years.

This -I- peak corresponding to the exchange of ambassadors is much larger than any since the founding of the current governments in these two countries. In viewing the -S- graph for PRC-India (Figure IV-7), note that at the date for announcing the exchange of ambassadors, there is no significant peak.

Early in 1984 in the PRC-India graph, there is a medium -S- peak as compared to the previous eight years. In early 1989 there is a peak higher than any in the previous forty years. Their combined-I- values are low at these times. Before commenting, it is best to consider the individual -S- graphs for the PRC, India and USSR.

Observe the very significant -S- period (shown in Figure IV-8) for the PRC in 1972-74. During this time the PRC made very significant diplomatic and economic advances. President Nixon of the US visited the PRC in February of 1972. The PRC had just been admitted to the United Nations on September 9, 1971, which opened the doors for an increased level of exchanges with the world during 1972-74. The high peak in late 1973 occurred at the time of the Arab-Israel war of 1973, and the related OPEC oil embargo and price rise, which adversely affected the PRC's efforts to open economic and diplomatic doors in the world.

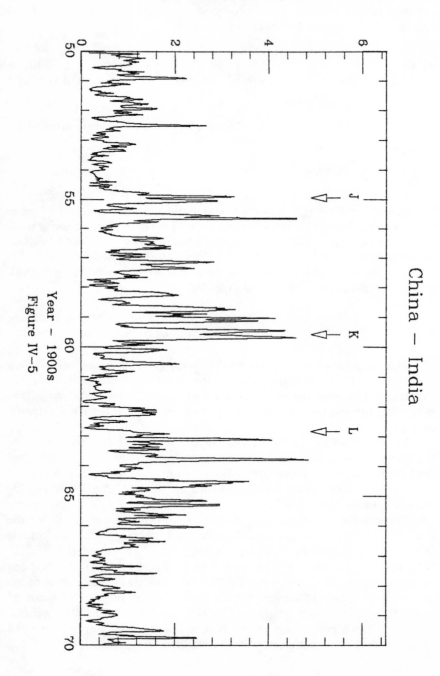

-S-
Intensity of Changes

China — India

Year — 1900s
Figure IV-5

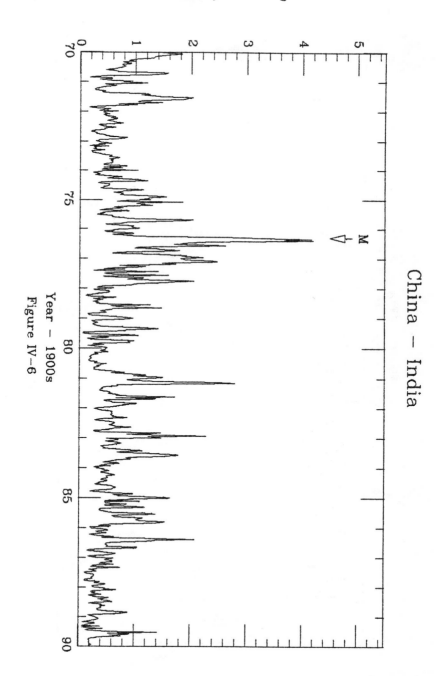

–I–
Intensity of Changes

China – India

Year – 1900s
Figure IV–6

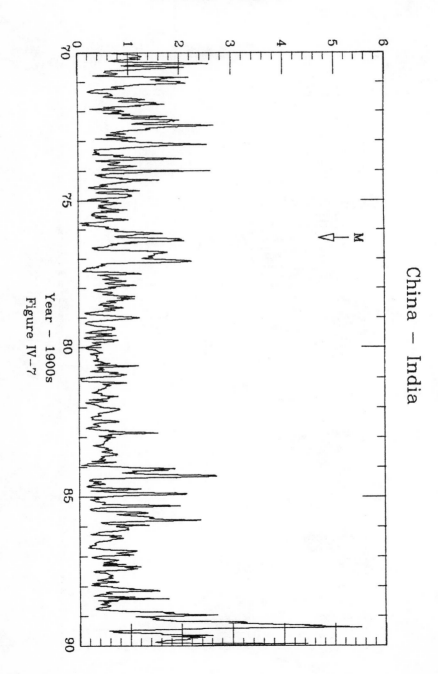

−S−

Intensity of Changes

China — India

Year − 1900s

Figure IV−7

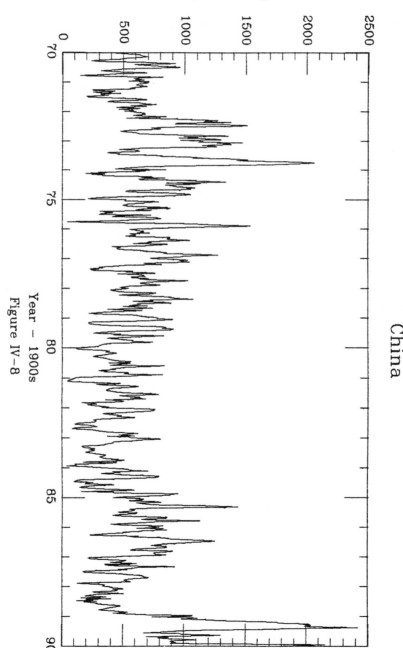

-S-

Intensity of Changes

China

Year — 1900s

Figure IV-8

India and Pakistan were "born" within hours of each other much to the disapproval of their astrologers. Their war and several other events for India are given below (Figure IV-9).

N	11-22-1971	India and Pakistan go to war.
O	12-1973	Arab-Israel war and OPEC oil-price rise.
P	5-18-1974	India explodes its first nuclear device.
Q	6-30-1975	State of emergency declared by Indira Gandhi.
R	3-20-1977	Indira Gandhi and Congress party's loss of power to Janata party.

The stress shown in late 1970 and early 1971 for India turned to war with Pakistan (event N). As with the PRC, the change in the price of oil in the world in 1973 immediately affected oil-poor India (event O).

Both India and the PRC show medium height -S- peaks in 1984. Their highest peaks are in 1988 or early 1989. The 1984 peaks will be discussed in the chapters on World Banking and World Powers. I will defer the discussion of the 1988-89 peaks until the chapter on World Powers for reasons that will become obvious as the book progresses.

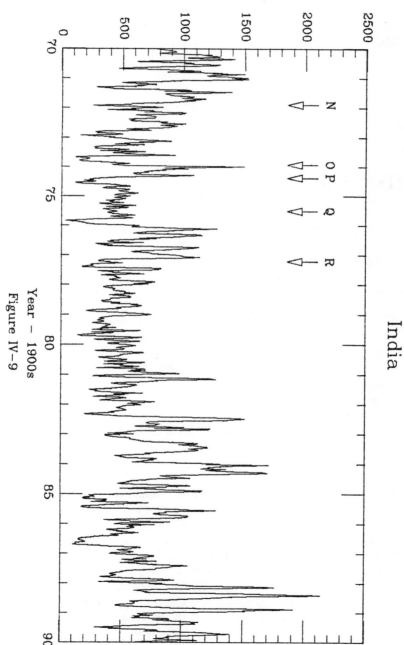

−S−
Intensity of Changes

India

Year − 1900s
Figure IV−9

CHAPTER V

MIDEAST

The Mideast can be conveniently thought of as consisting of three groups:

Group 1   The nations with large quantities of oil. For this group the representative nations will be Iran, Iraq, Libya and Saudi Arabia.

Group 2   The nations with little or no oil that border Israel and who fight wars with Israel. These nations are Egypt, Jordan, Lebanon and Syria.

Group 3   Israel.

Historically all of these nations or areas have followed a certain pattern of events this century:

1900 to World War I   These territories or nations were under the control of either France or Great Britain or a few other nations at brief times.

Post World War I to World War II   A wave of nationalism occurred as new monarchies and "republics" were set up and borders were defined or adjusted by France or Great Britain and the local political powers. There was a significant influx of Jewish settlers who purchased their land in the Palestine region from Arabs who were largely unfamiliar with European ways. The Jewish settlers began setting up a society which was technologically and culturally very different from that of their Arab neighbors. Some of the Arab population resettled due to the influx of Jewish settlers. Also, large oil fields were discovered.

Post World War II to 1953	The nationalist wave near the end of World War II resulted in the creation of independent nations in the region including Israel. With the initial war of Israeli independence, the Arabs discovered that they were centuries behind in many areas of endeavor. The Arab nations expelled their Jewish populations after the Israeli war of independence, and the oil companies began extensive development of the oil fields.
1953 to 1979	The overthrow of the monarchy in Egypt was the keystone of a new wave of nationalism. The monarchies in Iraq and Libya also fell as well as governments in Lebanon and Syria. In the Arab-Israeli wars of 1956, 1967 and 1973, as well as in their daily skirmishes, the Arabs discovered that having modern weapons did not make their nations modern.
1974 to 1979	Following the Arab-Israeli war of late 1973, the oil-producing nations took control of their oil and became very rich.
1979 to the present	The fusion of religion, oil, money and politics in Iran provided enough energy to overthrow the corrupt previous government. The repressive and dogmatic new government in Iran was, and is, not well received by most of the nations of the world, be they Islamic or not. The Gulf area nations turned their directions politically to compensate for this new development. The world economy also began to sour at this time.

We will begin our analysis by looking at the relations between Israel (Group 3) and its neighbors (Group 2) as seen in their combined -S- graphs. We will defer the discussion of the oil-producing (Group 1) nations until the time period 1970-89 is discussed. The following events are labeled in the 1950-69 combined -S- graphs:

A   10-29-1956   Egypt and Israel go to war.

B   9-28-1961   Execution of Adolf Eichmann.

           5-31-1962   *Coup d'etat* in Syria and breakup of United
                              Arab Republic, UAR.

C   6-5-1967   An Arab-Israeli war.

The related -S- graphs are as follows: Egypt-Israel in Figure V-1; Israel-Lebanon-Syria in Figure V-2; and Israel-Jordan in Figure V-3. The corresponding -I- graphs and the graphs for the other nations in the area are also of interest and I recommend that those readers interested in the Mideast obtain these numerous graphs from one of the sources indicated in the back of this book. The -S- graphs shown will serve adequately for our discussion.

The highest peak in the combined -S- graph for Egypt and Israel occurs just a few months after the Egypt-Israel war of 1956 (event A). In July 1956 Egypt's President Nasser had nationalized the Suez Canal and prevented Israeli-bound ships from using the canal. As tensions mounted in the region, Israel launched an offensive (event A). The stress coming shortly after the war is indicative of the repercussions from the war. France, Great Britain, the US and the UN became involved in the situation. The military's prominence in Israel increased. The Egyptians had a dramatic lesson on how poorly prepared they were to participate in the modern world. The big powers forced an Israeli withdrawal from the captured territories; Egypt to open the Suez Canal to Israeli shipping; and the stationing of UN forces between the two countries. Another wave of Arab nationalism quickly swept the region in the war's aftermath and on January 1, 1958, Egypt and Syria joined to form the UAR.

The ongoing stressful and changing situation between Egypt and Israel as seen in their combined graph corresponds to both internal and external events. For example, Egypt's attempt at a pan-nationalistic union with Syria in the UAR came to an end with a military *coup d' etat* (event B) as the stress level rose again in the Egypt-Israel -S- graph. Israel brought the holocaust, one of Israel's reasons to be, to the forefront of its awareness by executing Adolf Eichmann on May 31, 1962.

The timing of the breakup of the UAR is also seen in the Israel-Lebanon-Syria -S- graph (Figure V-2). There have been many coups in the Mideast. The significance of this one is that it stopped the pan-Arab movement for a time and resulted in major realignments in the Mideast as regards to ties to the US and USSR. Also, early 1962 saw another coup in Syria and additional ones followed in subsequent years.

During the 1961-62 time period, there was additional instability in the world political situation. Atmospheric testing of nuclear weapons was at its peak in late 1961. The Cuban missile crisis and Congo military actions occurred in late 1962. The situation could have been more stressful, but the world kept

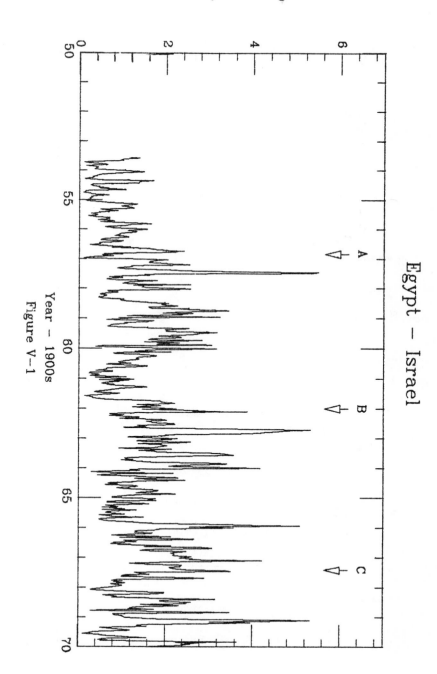

-S-
Intensity of Changes

Egypt – Israel

Year – 1900s

Figure V–1

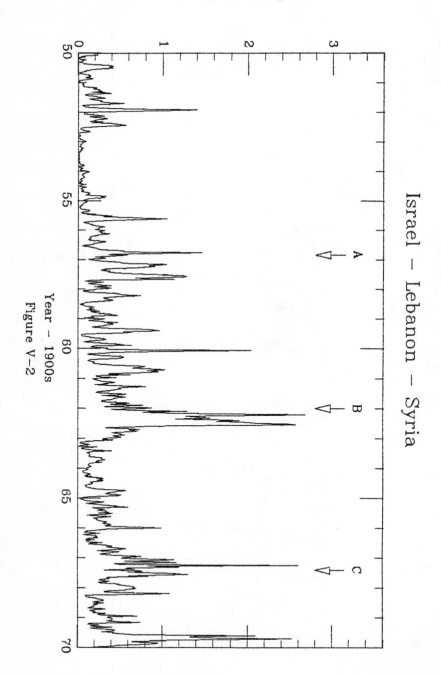

−S−

Intensity of Changes

Israel − Lebanon − Syria

Year − 1900s

Figure V−2

itself together. Two astrological keys to this were:

1) The -I- graphs of many nations of the world showed significant strength in 1962.
2) While all of the inner planets out to Saturn were in the sign of Aquarius, the three outer planets were neither making strong aspects with each other nor with very many of the inner planets (suggesting not a lot of activity).

The 1967 Arab-Israeli war is not particularly well marked in the Egypt-Israel combined -S- graph, but then Egypt was not the big loser; Jordan and Syria were. The combined Israel-Jordan -S- graph is shown in Figure V-3. On the single large peak in this graph (event C), Jordan changed by losing to Israel its portion of Jerusalem and the region known as the West Bank. This was Jordan's first war with Israel, since the war at the time of the formation of Israel, although the Palestine refugee groups had carried out border raids for years.

There had been fighting along Syria's border with Israel during most of the early part of 1967 where the large -S- peak is observed (Figure V-2). With the 1967 war coming just after the peak, Syria changed by losing the Golan Heights region. The problems coming from the loss of these regions by Jordan and Syria have not yet been resolved. Israel and Jordan have not yet made peace, and Israel and Syria have had further wars.

Both the Egypt-Israel and the Israel-Lebanon-Syria combined -S- graphs show significant strengths in 1969. Israel fought against Egypt along the Suez Canal zone and some Palestinian Liberation Organization (PLO) groups carried out hijackings which involved Syria. The PLO groups in Lebanon expanded their living areas amid conflicts with Lebanese groups. Iraq, the PLO and Syria all had troop concentrations in Jordan. In other words, the situation in the Mideast was at its norm for the period: intense changes via stressful politics and warfare. To survive, many of the groups in the Mideast had to quickly learn new political and military skills.

Moving now to the next two decades, we will look at the Dynamic Astrology graphs for the oil-producing Mideast nations (Group 1), the Arab neighbors of Israel (Group 2) and Israel (Group 3). Then we will also look at some of the combined graphs for Israel and Group 2 nations. The events labeled in all of these graphs are listed below:

D	Spring 1971	King Hussein of Jordan puts down the PLO and takes control of the territories of his country not in Israeli hands.
E	6-1-1972	Iraq nationalizes its oil.
F	10-6-1973	Egypt and Syria attack Israel and are quickly defeated. The Arab oil embargo follows along with the nationalization of the oil fields.

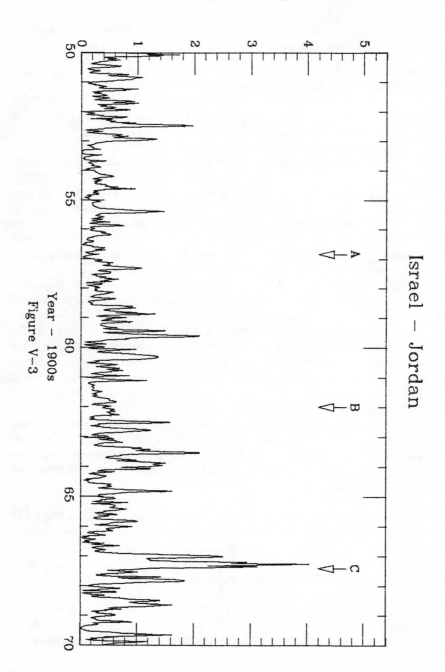

-S-
Intensity of Changes

Israel – Jordan

Year – 1900s
Figure V–3

G	2-22-1976	Egypt and Israel begin a partial withdrawal of forces in the Sinai. The agreements to do this were made in November of 1975.
	Spring 1975, Winter and Spring 1976	Lebanese civil war. Syria and the PLO take control of much of Lebanon.
H	11-19-1977	Egypt president Sadat visits Israel.
I	2-1-1979	Khomeini arrives in Tehran as the Shah's government falls.
	3-26-1979	Egypt and Israel sign Camp David accords, "Peace Treaty" in Washington, D.C.
J	11-04-1979 11-20-1979	US Embassy in Tehran is seized by militants. Grand Mosque in Mecca is taken over by Islamic militants.
K	9-22-1980	Iran-Iraq war begins.
L	6-6-1982	Israel's "incursion" into Lebanon begins.

In the spring of 1971 (event D) King Hussein of Jordan had to fight the PLO for control of his country. This event does not appear as a major peak in the -I- or -S- graphs for Jordan (not shown). This means that Jordan was not prepared to make the changes that a PLO-dominated government would entail. However, there is a Dynamic Astrology -S- graph that is very interesting to consider. The establishment of the Hashemite rule by Abdullah ibn Hussein in Amman, Transjordan, occurred on April 1, 1921. The -S- graph calculated for this event has a higher value (in the spring of 1921) than any value for almost seventy years thereafter. King Hussein was able to use his talents and his country's disinclination to change to hold his throne and emerge a more powerful leader.

Oil has helped focus world attention on the Mideast. Up until the 1970s, the Mideast's oil was controlled by the industrialized nations of the West. The combined -S- graphs are shown in Figure V-4 for the oil-producing nations (Group 1). The sharp -S- peak in 1972 corresponds to event E. Pressures were building in the Mideast for national control of the oil production. The price of oil was very low compared to its true value in world commerce. Iraq took advantage of its situation by taking complete control of its oil fields. The Iraqis had learned enough to try operating the fields and their oil profits themselves.

This act increased the pressure on all of the oil-producing nations to

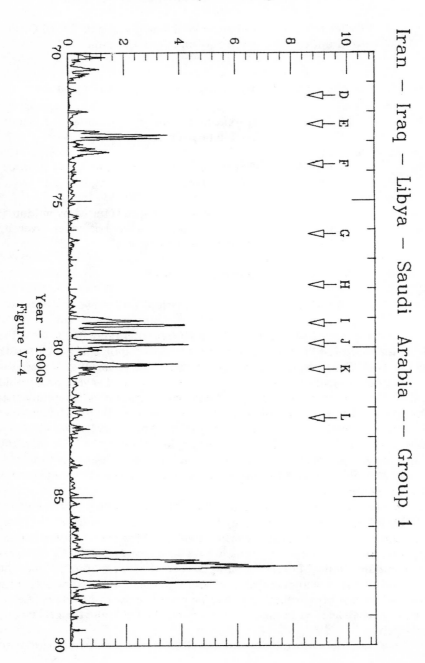

-S-
Intensity of Changes

Iran – Iraq – Libya – Saudi Arabia –– Group 1

Year – 1900s
Figure V–4

more rapidly take control of their oil. They intensified negotiations to get 51% control of the relevant companies, and the months rolled by.

Egypt and Syria attacked Israel in late 1973. There is a very high -S- peak in Israel's -S- graph (Figure V-5) for this war (event F). Israel almost lost the war, but when it was over, Israel had taken most of the Sinai. In response, the oil-producing nations had an inspiration. They would stop delivering oil to those Western industrial nations who they felt had supported Israel. The high -I- peak (event F) in their combined -I- graphs (Figure V-6) corresponds to this decision. However, the inspiration went much farther. By the end of 1974 this group had not 51% control of their oil but 100% control, and the oil prices had dramatically escalated.

The organizational tool for this process was OPEC, which is discussed in the next chapter. The OPEC nations had been learning not only from Israel but also from the industrialized West. They had learned, to a degree, that political and social power can be achieved without warfare. The OPEC nations raised prices and accumulated vast revenues. However, their overindulgent price raises did not stop over the years and the consequences began to arrive in 1978 as indicated in their -S- graph (Figure V-4).

Before getting to the late 1978 changes in the Mideast, look at Figures V-7 and V-8. Here the combined -I- and -S- graphs are shown for the Arab nations (Group 2) that study politics, technology and warfare with Israel. The highest -I- peak for Group 2 was in early 1974, just after the 1973 war (event F). Clearly, the idea of profiting by nationalizing the oil was supported by the Group 2 nations as well as the Group 1 nations. The oil money also flowed to these confrontation states via secondary channels.

A second major -I- peak occurred in 1975 (Figure V-7 of the Group 2 nations). Two events occurred (event G). Egypt began negotiations for Israeli withdrawal from the Sinai; the PLO and Syria began their attempt to take over Lebanon. The Egypt-Israeli relations are more clearly seen in Figure V-9 (where their combined -I- values are shown). The highest -I- peak for this time period corresponds to event G. With this event, Egypt and Israel were set on a course of cooperation which culminated a few years later (events H and I) with Sadat's visit to Israel and the Camp David accords. Note that this change in circumstances for Israel was also very stressful (Figure V-5). The -S- value is at its maximum for the twenty-year period when in November of 1975 the Sinai withdrawal agreements were signed (event G).

The second event that started with the 1975 -I- peak in the Group 2 graph (Figure V-7) is the civil war in Lebanon. The Arab defeat in the 1973 war with Israel brought added pressure on the PLO. Although for different reasons, the PLO and Syria decided to take over Lebanon, which was a thriving commercial center on the Mediterranian. Various religiously oriented groups, some with Israel's support, also wanted a bigger piece of the action in Lebanon. Their inspirations (Figure V-7) of 1975 turned into very stressful violence in 1976 when Syria invaded Lebanon as part of the civil war. (See

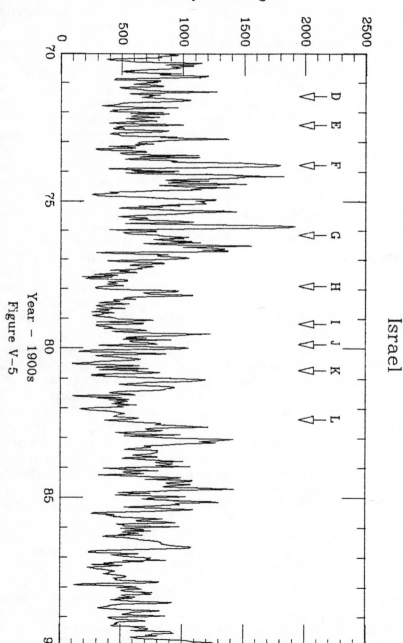

Figure V-5

Year – 1900s

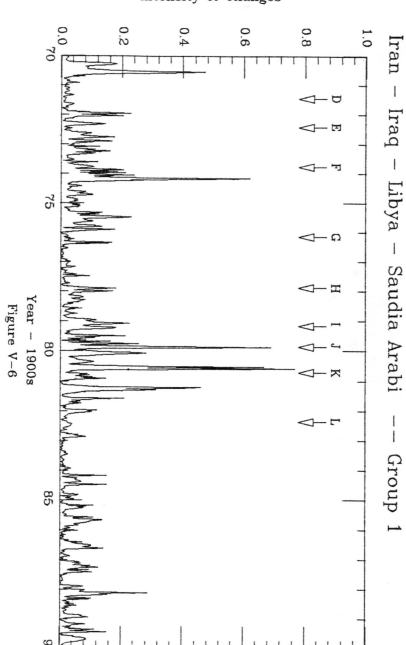

-I-
Intensity of Changes

Iran — Iraq — Libya — Saudia Arabi — — Group 1

Year — 1900s

Figure V-6

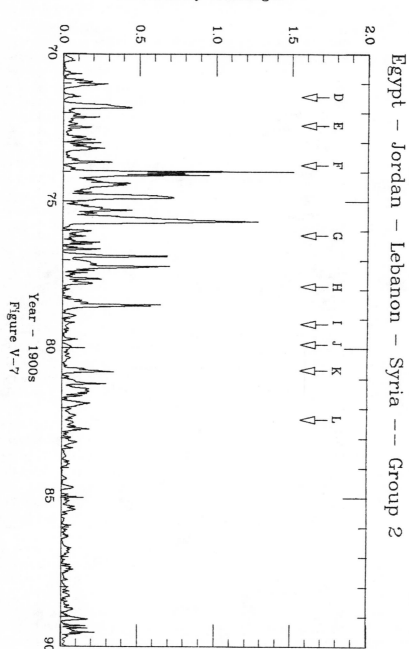

−I−
Intensity of Changes

Egypt – Jordan – Lebanon – Syria –– Group 2

Year – 1900s

Figure V–7

event G in Figure V-10 of the -S- values for Israel-Labanon-Syria.) Lebanon
was ground into pieces.

The consequences of Egypt's and Israel's coming peaceably together and
the Lebanese civil war are seen in the high level for late 1976 and all of 1977
in the Group 2 combined -S- graph (Figure V-8). Note also Figure V-10 for
Israel-Lebanon-Syria. As stated above, Anwar Sadat, president of Egypt, went
to Israel. That the leader of the nation which had fought Israel in all of its
wars should make peace with Israel, demonstrated that a new level of achieve-
ment had been reached by the rapidly evolving Arab nations. The event was
stressful but had begun with great inspiration (event G in Figures V-7 and
V-9). Note also that the combined Egypt-Israel -S- graph (not shown for this
time period) does not show any significant stress for this event. The stress
was among the other Arab nations and in Israel.

Returning now to the oil-producing nations (Group 1, Figures V-4 and
V-6), observe that the events involving Egypt, Israel, Lebanon, Jordan and
Syria had little influence toward changes in the oil-producing nations. The
activity of spending the profits from their rapidly rising oil income to build
up their nations was keeping them occupied. Their combined -I- and -S- graphs
do not show any new peaks until late 1978. Then the -S- graph shows a set
of three peaks starting in late 1978 corresponding to events I, J and K, and
their -I- graph has peaks at events J and K.

Many groups in the Mideast wanted a piece of the action in oil money.
The Shah of Iran had lost touch with his people, but the religious leaders
had not. With the fall of the Shah and the ascent of Khomeini, oil money
was fused with religion and politics on the first of the three peaks (event I).
With the next peak (event J in Figures V-4 and V-6) in late 1979 the militants
took the US Embassy in Tehran and the Grand Mosque in Mecca. The leaders
of the oil nations wondered if they were next to fall while they quickly moved
to get political support from their lower classes and religious elements in their
countries.

For these peaks in 1978-80, the third one in Figure V-4 and the second
one in Figure V-6 correspond to Event K. At this time, two key members of
OPEC, Iran and Iraq, went to war. The war was initially an attempt by Iraqis
to stop their historical enemy, Iran, from spreading its religious fanaticism
at what was considered an opportune time. Further, the war was to gain
valuable territories and prestige for the Iraqi leaders. The result was that both
of the countries sustained significant damage to their oil fields and the war
goes on today.

The events of 1979 are also seen as a major peak in the -S- graph for
the Group 2 nations (Figure V-8). Islamic fundamentalism and the inspiration to form Islamic republics were, and are, an issue for all of the nations
with large Muslim populations.

The recent Israeli "incursion" into Lebanon (event L) is seen (Figure V-5)
as a medium peak. A half year later, in early 1983, there is a higher peak,
the highest in the last six years. The "incursion" itself was not as stressful

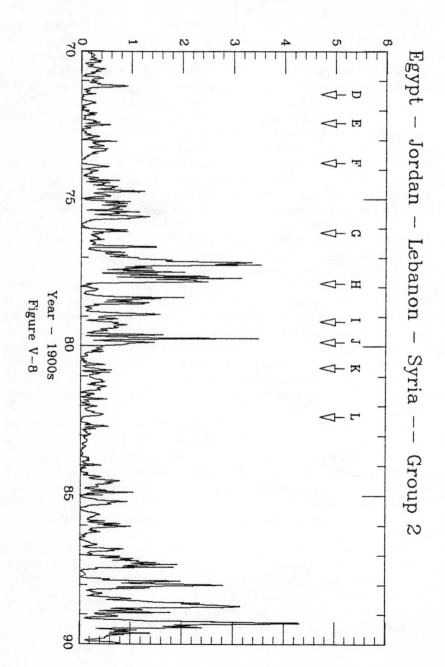

-S-
Intensity of Changes

Egypt – Jordan – Lebanon – Syria –– Group 2

Year – 1900s
Figure V-8

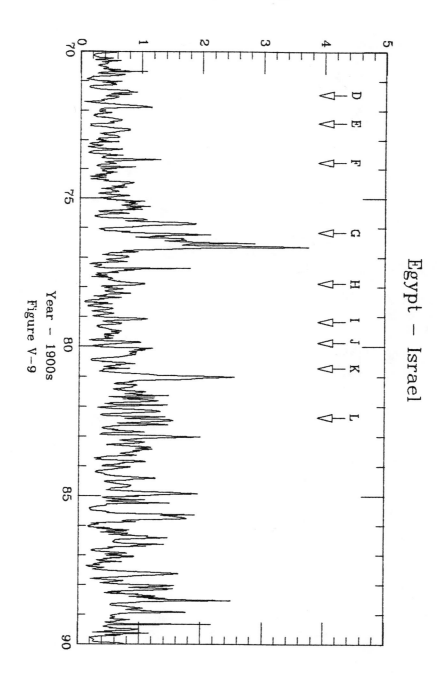

-I-
Intensity of Changes

Egypt – Israel

Year – 1900s
Figure V-9

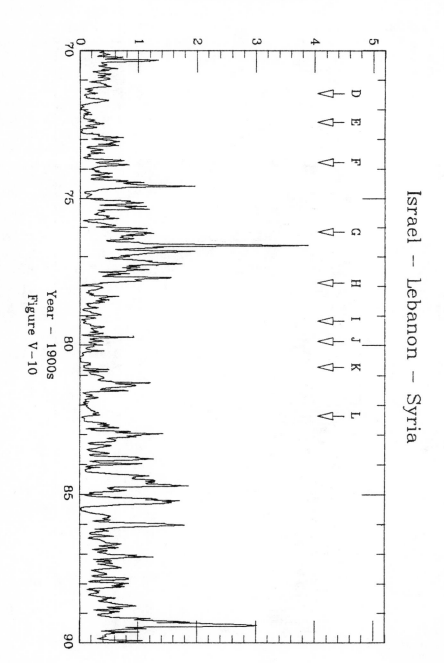

-S-
Intensity of Changes

Israel – Lebanon – Syria

Year – 1900s
Figure V–10

to Israel as were the political problems in early 1983 coming from the massacre of civilians in Lebanon. If we look at the combined Israel-Lebanon -I- graph (Figure V-11), we observe that there is a step increase in the -I- values beginning in 1982. The Israeli "incursion" into Lebanon appears in part as a cooperative venture between some elements that created the Lebanese government and Israel. Of course, being the Mideast, the usual level of violence was involved and there is no immediate prospect for a resolution of the consequences of the "incursion."

The political and religious environment in the Mideast today operates at a point of development where the evolution often comes out of the barrel of a gun. This has not always been the case, as the records of ancient wisdom show us. Remember, evolvement occurs at all levels, however violent or peaceful. This observation is not intended to excuse the present violence in the Mideast, but to point out that it is not impossible that lessons are being learned that will lead to something more aware and loving eventually taking place in the region.

The high peaks in 1987-89 will be discussed in the chapter on World Powers.

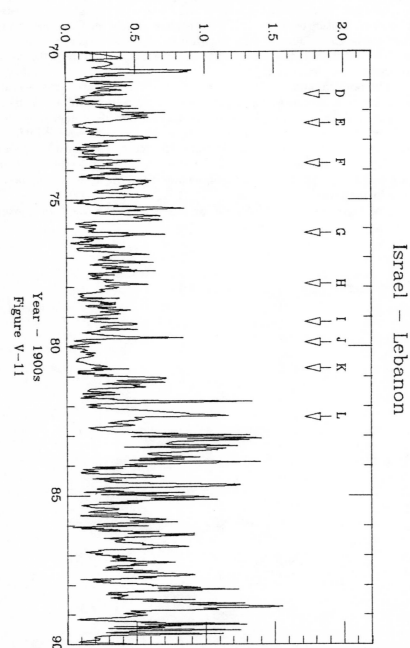

−I−

Intensity of Changes

Israel – Lebanon

Year – 1900s

Figure V–11

CHAPTER VI
WORLD BANKING

Bretton Woods

In the summer of 1944, with World War II at its height of intensity and glimmers of the Allies' success on the horizon, key bankers of the world met at Bretton Woods, New Hampshire. They made plans for establishment of the International Monetary Fund (IMF) and a separate institution, the International Bank for Reconstruction and Development. With the establishing of these two institutions, the Bretton Woods Conference set the monetary framework for the postwar recovery and the tremendous economic expansion of the nations of the world during the next several decades. Two "birth dates" are used to make the graphs for the IMF: the first is the last day of the conference when the agreements were signed and the second is after the war when the money was first deposited into the IMF.

During the 1950s and 1960s the IMF grew slowly. Though it did not channel a very large fraction of the world's financial resources, it did operate as a kind of regulator for world banking. The mechanism for this regulation is that IMF funds come from deposits by nations, thereby interconnecting the monetary policies of the member nations. By receiving loans from the IMF, the borrowing nations' monetary policies and economies also became connected to the world banking system. From the point of view of those nations receiving loans, the IMF was and is important for their economic, social and political development. From the point of view of the lending nations, the IMF is an important tool to expand world commerce while stabilizing monetary policies.

In the late 1960s and early 1970s the IMF decided to expand. One of the methods of expansion was the creation of special drawing rights (SDRs). The SDRs did not prove to be as effective as hoped for in the expansion of the IMF. However, events in the early 1970s resulted in alternative funds being available to expand the IMF's sources of funds to loan.

To continue to investigate the colorful life of the IMF, we will use the
-I- and -S- graphs (Figures VI-1 and VI-2) for 1970-89. The following events
are labeled:

A	8-15-1971	The US ceases to back the dollar with gold.
B	2-12-1973 and 3-01-1973 to 3-19-1973	Closing of international money exchange markets due to high world inflation and problems with the US dollar followed by the floating of currencies.
C	10-06-1973	Arab-Israel war of 1973.
D	9-22-1980	Iran-Iraq war, still in progress, or disprogress as the case may be.

Heavy speculation in the US dollar brought the US to stop backing the dollar
with gold (event A). There are medium peaks for this event in both the -I-
and -S- graphs. With the dollar and the other major currencies of the world
floating, 1972 was a very stressful year for the world's monetary systems. This
correlates with the very high peaks in the -S- graphs. Early 1973 was no better and on the high peak in the -S- graph the money markets were closed
(event B). Due to these and other difficulties, the SDRs were not working
out as well as originally hoped. Also, most currencies in the world began floating relative to the dollar in the spring of 1973.

This state of affairs was radically altered when in the wake of the 1973
Arab-Israel war, OPEC began rapidly raising the price of oil on the world
market. Very quickly the OPEC nations accumulated unprecedented surpluses
of cash, some of which was channeled through the IMF. Major commercial
banks or groups thereof also handled many of the resulting loans. However,
these banks did not want too large a fraction of their portfolios tied to too
few lending or borrowing countries. As a consequence, the IMF and other
international banks were frequently involved in large consortium loans that
had connections to the commercial banks. The IMF made use of its 1971,
and later its 1978, large increases in quotas (deposits by member nations) for
its share of the action. The interconnections between the monetary systems
of the nations of the world increased.

The happy flow of money

1) from the nations of the world,
2) to the OPEC nations,
3) through the banks,
4) into loans and
5) then back to the nations of the world

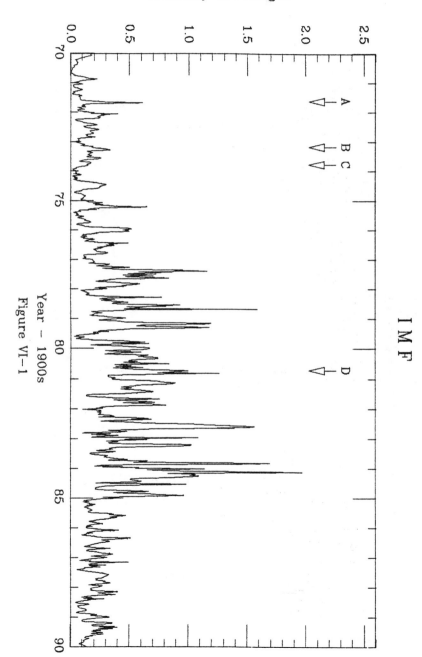

−I−
Intensity of Changes

I M F

Year – 1900s
Figure VI-1

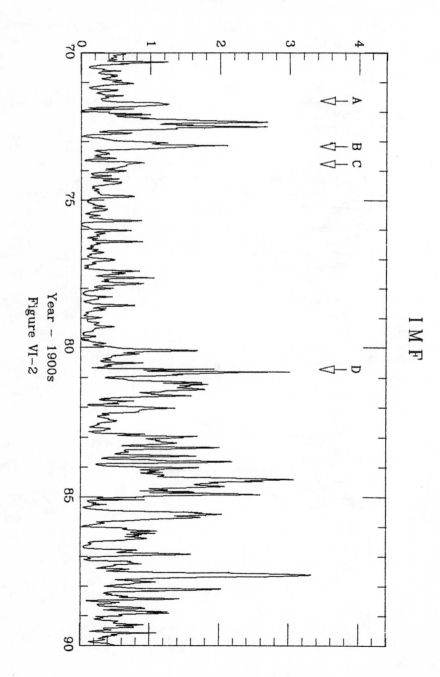

-S-
Intensity of Changes

Figure VI-2

is seen by the rising values in the IMF -I- graph and the low -S- values during the mid and late 1970s. With the loans, many developing nations began huge projects. The OPEC nations spent vast amounts of their oil revenues on development projects and military hardware. The industrial nations that were able to keep their expenditures for oil low, made large profits from the sale of goods that were either purchased with the loans or oil revenue. In some cases the developing countries' projects had the desired effect of increasing the productivity of the country, thereby allowing the loans to be repaid.

The difficulties began in 1980, following the second of the large increases in oil prices by OPEC in 1979. The new loans to the borrowing nations were almost all going to pay the interest on the old loans. This meant that the borrowing nations purchased less goods from the industrialized nations. Energy — i.e., oil — use in the world declined. Non-OPEC nations that produced oil took an increasingly larger share of the oil market. At event D, two of the major OPEC nations went to war with each other on a high IMF -S- peak (Figure VI-2). International banking continued to find innovative solutions to these challenges (Figure VI-1). The situation in mid-1983 is that the price of oil on the world market has dropped significantly but the banking system is holding together. Many nations have rescheduled their loans. The total of international loans is approaching $700 billion in 1983. The discussion of the time from mid-1983 on will be given in the summary section of this chapter.

Organization of Petroleum Exporting Countries

Because of its importance to world banking, it is instructive to look at OPEC's -I- and -S- graphs (Figures VI-3 and VI-4). The Arab-Israel war of 1973 (event C) appears as a major peak in the -I- graph. Since OPEC is mostly comprised of Arab nations, it is not surprising that an Arab war would appear in the graph. In the aftermath of the war on this inspirational peak, the OPEC nations began the large increases in oil prices. Additional discussion of this event is given in Chapter V.

The highest -I- peak in the OPEC graph has a broad base that almost completely covers the year 1978. The world was in a slight recession and inflation was also high. OPEC decided to raise prices. The increased profits, as usual, were put into new international loans to third-world countries via the world banking system. As is discussed above, the result is that world productivity has not significantly increased and over 90% of new international loans are going to pay interest on the old loans. The other significant event of late 1978 was the fall of the Shah of Iran, a non-Arab OPEC nation. Other political groups within the OPEC nations want(ed) a bigger share of the money coming in and the resultant political power. Some of these groups' initiatives and inspirations succeeded in Iran.

The next war related to OPEC was stressful in character and is seen in the -S- values of the OPEC graph (Figure VI-4). Two OPEC members, Iran

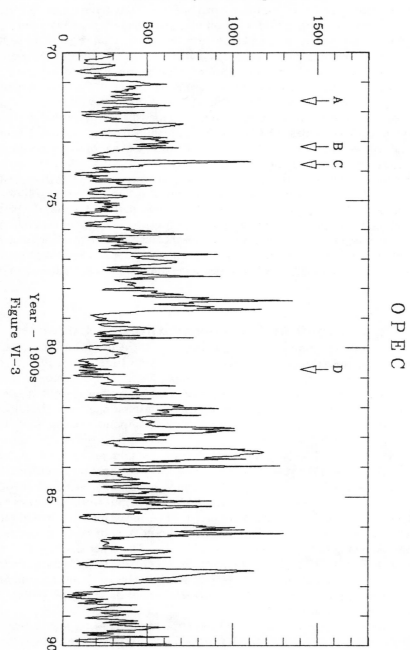

-I-
Intensity of Changes

OPEC

Year - 1900s
Figure VI-3

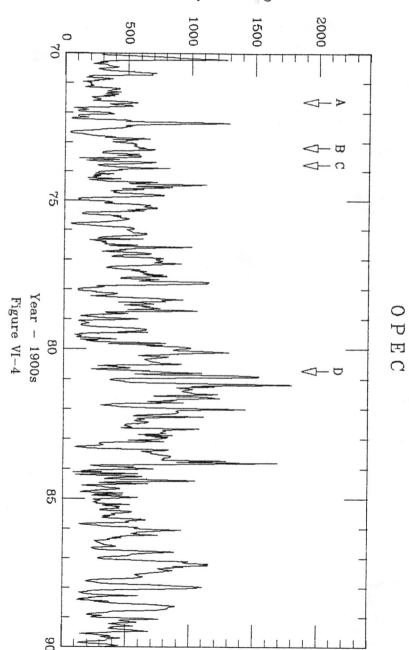

−S−
Intensity of Changes

OPEC

A

B C

D

Year − 1900s
Figure VI-4

and Iraq, went to war (event D) and destroyed much of each others' oil fields. The OPEC -S- curve was a few months away from its maximum for the twenty-year period.

The high stress level of changes indicated in the OPEC -S- graph during the early 1980s relates not only to the Iran-Iraq war but also to the disarray in OPEC. The member nations no longer agree on prices and quotas. OPEC oil production is off significantly. Oil prices are dropping, which will result in loan repayment difficulties for some nations.

European Economic Community

Noting that Europe, with the US, operates most of the world's banking, it is interesting to look at the European Economic Community (EEC), often called the Common Market. Figures VI-5 and VI-6 show the -I- and -S- graphs for the EEC which come from two dates of birth: the treaty signed in Rome setting up the EEC and the day for the start of the EEC. The -I- graph for the EEC shows medium and high -I- values from 1972 through 1985. So far, during this time the EEC has been growing beyond the areas of commerce to become the structure on which the movement towards European unity has been launched. The highest -I- peak for this time period was in 1975. During that year the plans were set for the election of a European Parliament. European Councils were instituted and work was begun on setting up European passports for Community citizens. The European Parliament elections took place in June 1979, and its first meeting occurred in July 1979. During the 1970s the EEC expanded its membership, and, equally important for the EEC, it did not lose any members.

Summary: 1984 and Beyond

All of the -I- and -S- graphs shown in this chapter show very high peaks in late 1983 or 1984. For the IMF -I- and EEC -S- graphs, these peaks are the highest peaks for the twenty-year period shown. The inference is simple: in late 1983 or 1984 the largely oil-financed international banking system will go through a major change involving creatively meeting stressful challenges.

I have made the above statement with pleasant sounding words. Obviously the radical alterations in the economic situation in the world in 1984 will result in great difficulties for many of the peoples and nations. Human society has clearly chosen this time to face the challenges involved in creating a world economic system. As economics lead to politics, the world in this time of great change is also dealing with the question of setting up a world political system.

Observe that while the big changes in world banking and commerce will occur in late 1983 and 1984, there are some changes indicated for 1987 (Figure VI-2); 1986-87 (Figure VI-3); and 1985 (Figure VI-5).

Finally, to return to the banking system only, it needs to be noted that the world banking system, as it exists today, was set up in the precomputer era. In the late 1970s computers and their associated software began to be

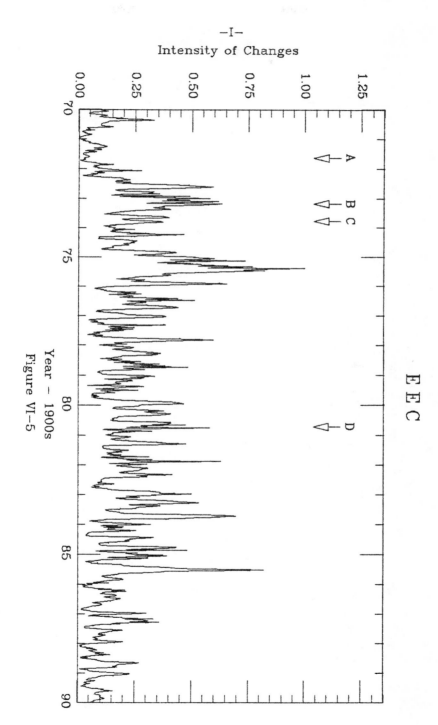

Intensity of Changes

−I−

Year − 1900s

Figure VI−5

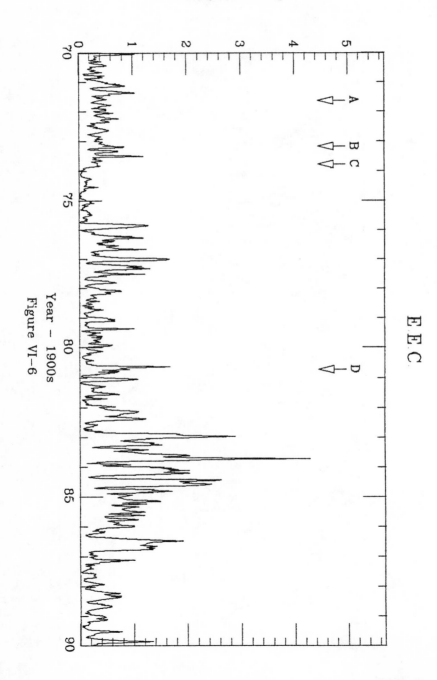

-S-
Intensity of Changes

E E C

Year – 1900s
Figure VI-6

powerful enough to attempt modeling the economy of the world. It is possible that the post 1984 world banking system will be managed by the results
obtained with the new computer models. However, at the present time the
computer-based models are not viewed very favorably by the banking community. One of the reasons is that in the late 1960s and early 1970s these
models were oversold before they were ready.

Even if computer models are used extensively for banking in the future,
the quality of the world's banking system will still depend on the quality of
the people involved. People write the programs; people build the computers;
and people interpret and carry out the results. The point is that there are ways
to improve world commerce and banking, whether with computers or other
means, and the world is about to try some of them, or at least terminate some
of the existing systems.

CHAPTER VII
NUCLEAR ENERGY AND SPACE

This century's developing nuclear energy and space programs provide us with a new kind of entity to investigate using Dynamic Astrology. The entities involved are not people, countries or institutions, but events: the first nuclear reactor, the first atom bomb, the first satellite, etc.

Historically there were three impetuses for the successful development of nuclear devices. The first two impetuses came from the US belief that nuclear fission weapons might be possible and that Germany was attempting to create them as part of their war effort during World War II. The third impetus came in the US response to the USSR development of fission nuclear weapons. The US felt the need to develop fusion weapons. In both of these situations some sources of motivation were related to mutual fears of domination and overly developed philosophies of competition. Considering what was taking place in Germany during World War II, some of the fears were justified. These situations correspond to the stages of development attained by these countries as presently incarnated. At further stages of evolvement, competition is used as an emotional tool rather than a quasi religion.

For our first group of entities, we will use the first atomic bomb tests of both the USSR and the US. In this way we will see the combined results of the tests themselves, the associated fears and the competitive elements. Specifically three detonations will be used:

1) The first plutonium atomic bomb was tested at the Trinity site in New Mexico.
2) The first uranium atomic bomb was tested by the US who dropped it on Hiroshima, Japan.
3) The first USSR atomic bomb was probably a plutonium device. These three events will be referred to as the Atomic Bomb Group (ABG).

For our discussion, the following events are labeled in the ABG Dynamic

Astrology graphs and in the subsequent graphs for the 1950-69 time period shown in this chapter:

A	11-1-1952	First hydrogen or fusion bomb explosion
B	10-4-1957	*Sputnik I*
C	10-30-1961	60-megaton USSR fusion bomb test
D	10-1962	Cuban missile crisis
E	10-10-1963	Atmospheric test ban treaty
F	1-22-1968	First Saturn launching of an Apollo module
G	7-20-1969	First human landing on the Moon

The highest -S- value in the ABG's graph (Figure VII-1) corresponds to the first fusion-bomb explosion (event A)! There are several -S- peaks observed just before the first fusion bomb as the fabricators struggled theoretically, technically and politically to achieve a viable fusion bomb. The USSR and US cold war was also under way.

Once the fusion bomb was achieved, notice that there were several years with relatively few changes indicated. Then *Sputnik I* was launched, (event B), on a medium peak. The launching of *Sputnik I* dramatically informed the world that nuclear weapons could be dropped anywhere on the Earth. As everyone who was a kid in school in the US at that time knows, meaningful and well-attended science classes started the day after *Sputnik I*. (Unfortunately, in the US today, science teachers have left the classrooms for better pay, working in government and industry with computers and their spin-offs. The US has relatively few good science teachers as compared to other industrialized nations. Furthermore, the students live with a ten-year-old legacy of antiscience feelings generated at the time of the Vietnam war.) The space programs developed rapidly, and along with the peaks seen in the years around 1960, there were numerous space firsts.

The highest -S- peak following the first fusion bomb shown in the ABG's graph corresponds to the largest fusion bomb ever exploded (event C). In fact, the explosion was much larger than planned for and the 60-megaton listing is only one of several guesses. For the world, the situation at that time was not a guess but a case of clear actions. The world outcry was enormous. The world had had enough. The late 1961 atmospheric tests of nuclear weapons were considered to be beyond the endurable limit and the atmospheric tests were stopped. Khrushchev of the USSR and Kennedy of the US played a few games with each other in Cuba (event D), but the atmospheric test ban treaty was signed a year later (event E). There are still a few countries that have

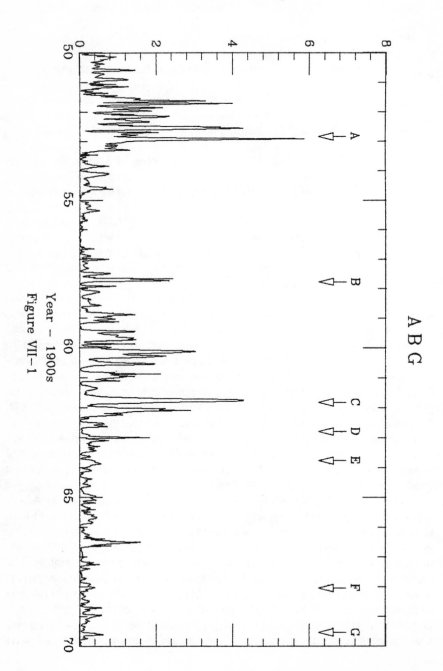

−S−
Intensity of Changes

Figure VII-1

not evolved enough to stop atmospheric testing of nuclear weapons. These tests are fortunately few in number. A comment in defense of the actions of these nations is that those nations with developed arsenals of nuclear weapons have done very little in recent years to relieve the fears of those nations without or with few nuclear weapons.

From late 1962 on, the -S- level of the ABG group has been low and, with the exception of a few medium or narrow peaks, remains low. The world has proved disinclined to try to blow itself up and has decided to provide itself with entertainment and creative expression through other avenues.

Shown in Figure VII-2 is the -I- graph for the ABG. The first significant peak is about a year before the launching of *Sputnik I*. The highest peak, (event F), is a year and a half before *Apollo 11* landed on the Moon (event G). This peak and the other -I- peaks may also relate to new nuclear weapons, the development of other missiles to be used to carry bombs or the related communications systems, but the public history or awareness of the relevant events is not clear enough to demonstrate this. What is more interesting is to follow the line of development of nuclear energy and space using a broader class of first events.

The sequence I have chosen to follow is:

1) The first nuclear reactor going critical.
2) The first atomic (fission) bomb explosion.
3) The first fusion bomb explosion.
4) The first launching of a satellite.

Clearly this sequence of events could be extended or a different line of scientific development followed. For that matter, artistic or musical development could be followed, but my purpose here is to give one example that will relate to most readers and stay with the example of nuclear energy and space. The concepts involved are generally applicable.

We will begin our analysis with the combined -I- and -S- graphs for the first reactor, atomic bomb and fusion bomb (Figures VII-3 and VII-4). The highest -I- peak corresponds to *Apollo 11's* landing on the Moon (event G)! The success of the landing on the Moon was due to the initiative, cooperation and imagination of the people involved. The second highest -I- peak is shortly before *Sputnik I's* launch (event B). Looking at the -S- graph, we observe one of the three highest -S- peaks to correspond exactly to the launching of *Sputnik I* and another to the first lunar landing. The highest of these three peaks is a few months before the first test of a killer satellite by the USSR on October 20, 1968, the first launching of a manned Apollo spacecraft, *Apollo 7*, October 11, 1968, and the first manned orbiting of the Moon, *Apollo 8*, December 21, 1968.

Numerous medium-sized peaks are also observed in Figures VII-3 and VII-4. The development of nuclear energy and space technology was paralleled

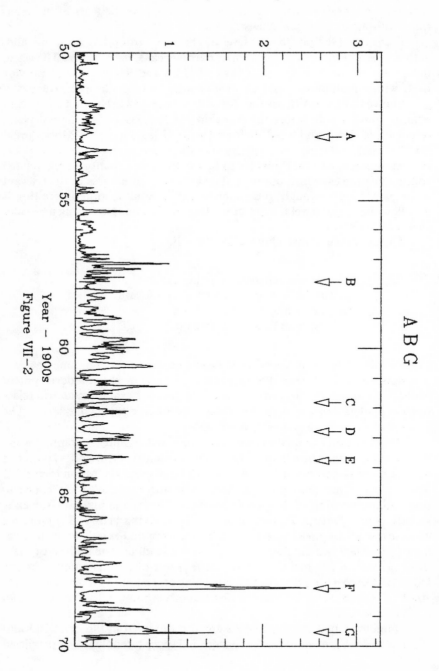

–I–
Intensity of Changes.

Figure VII-2

-I-
Intensity of Changes

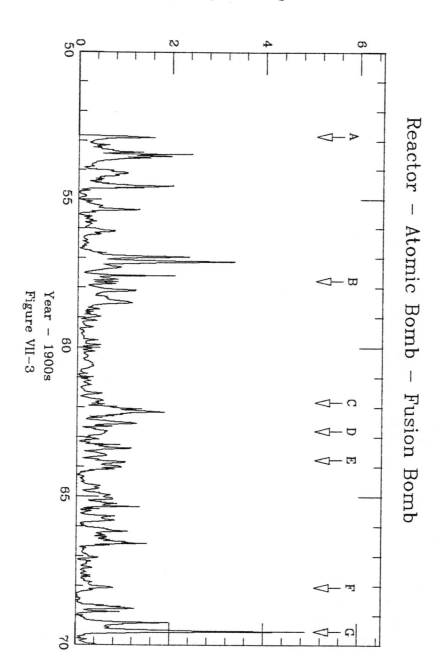

Reactor – Atomic Bomb – Fusion Bomb

Year – 1900s
Figure VII–3

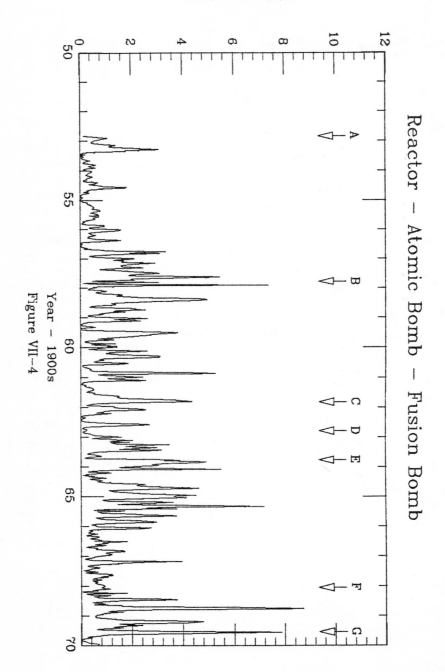

−S−
Intensity of Changes

Reactor − Atomic Bomb − Fusion Bomb

Year − 1900s

Figure VII−4

by, and relied upon, other developments in science and technology. To list a few: the first widely available digital computers came on the markets in the late 1950s and every few years thereafter their capacities have increased at an exponential rate; the first laser was made operational in the summer of 1960; and, the first manned space flight was on April 12, 1961.

If we now add the launching of *Sputnik I* to the list of events being combined, there are significant changes in the character of the graphs. In the -I- graph (Figure VII-5), the first lunar-landing peak height is reduced significantly. The highest -I- peak is just after the launching of *Sputnik I* when both the US and USSR made enormous increases in their space programs. In the -S- graph (Figure VII-6) the larger peaks are in the mid-1960s, with the highest peak at event E: the Atmospheric Test Ban Treaty.

These changes in the graphs can be understood by noting that *Sputnik I's* launch was an event that was set up by a different group of scientists, than the ones who created the first nuclear reactor, first atomic bomb and first fusion bomb, all US events. If you trace back the origins of the people who were working at NASA in the lunar-landing program, you will find that either they or their teachers had been members of these earlier US projects. The close connectedness of this group is why the -I- graph shown in Figure VII-3 has such high values! These events were astrologically tuned into each other as was, and is, the consciousnesses of the individuals involved. The *Sputnik I* event was created by a separate group of people in the USSR which was only loosely connected to the US scientists. The element of competition came in again as seen with the ABG results. The -I- graph is suppressed and the -S- graph shows the struggle in the mid 1960s between the USSR and US to dominate nuclear energy, space, and missile developments.

In the -S- graph (Figure VII-6) at the time of the Cuban missile crisis (event D) the -S- value is almost zero. At the signing of the Atmospheric Test Ban Treaty, the -S- value is at its maximum. Scientists had little to do directly with the Cuban missile crisis, but they had a significant impact on pushing for the treaty. Given the opportunity, scientists amid stress will make peace and try to create a new theory, experiment or device. Warfare is destructive to the activities which scientists use to generate their identity.

The -I- and -S- graphs for these four natal events are continued into the next two decades in Figures VII-7 and VII-8. One event is labeled in these graphs:

H   4-12-1981   First launching of the US space shuttle

On one of the higher combined -I- peaks to date, the first reusable human-operated and occupied space vehicle was launched into Earth orbit (event H). However, the highest -I- peak occurs in late 1977. It appears that the USSR made significant advances in directed-energy weapons and related magneto-hydrodynamics around this time. As many of the similar activities in the

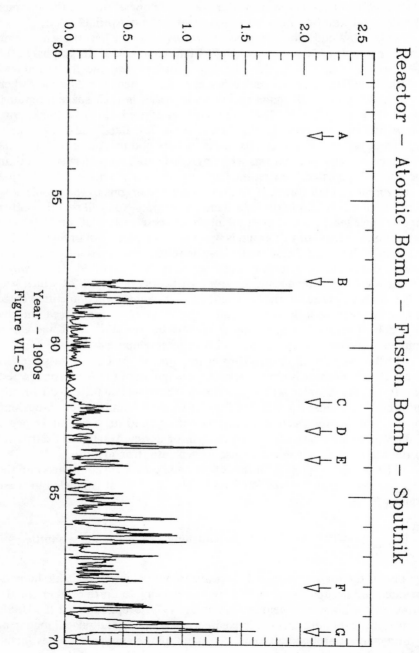

Reactor – Atomic Bomb – Fusion Bomb – Sputnik

Intensity of Changes

−I−

Year – 1900s

Figure VII–5

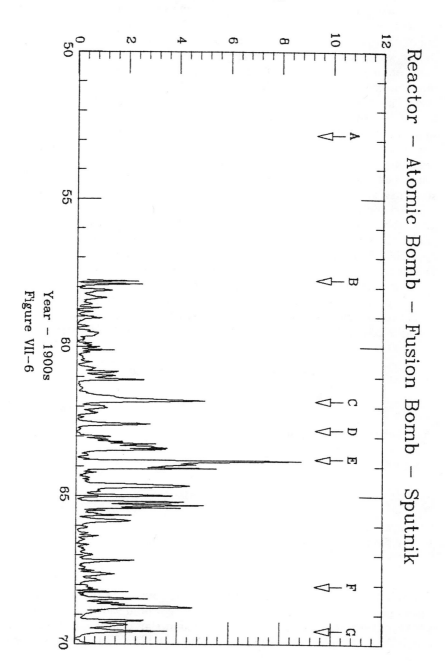

-S-
Intensity of Changes

Reactor – Atomic Bomb – Fusion Bomb – Sputnik

Year – 1900s
Figure VII-6

US are five to ten years behind and most of the developments are classified, relating the appropriate events is difficult. Otherwise, from 1970 up to event H, there are numerous medium-height -I- peaks (Figure VII-7) and in the combined -S- graph there are several very high -S- peaks (Figure VII-8). This period of time has seen global instant communications installed, mass marketing of micro computers, and so many other firsts of science and technology that it would take an encyclopedia just to catalog them.

Looking now to the near future, with the exception of one or maybe two medium-sized -S- peaks, the -S- values are relatively low from 1980 through 1989. The -I- values in 1984 and 1985, after two years of very low values following the first space shuttle launch, achieve high values again, and then return to medium and then low values. The implications for nuclear energy, space and possibly some of the related electronic fields are that the world is busy installing what has already been developed in the sense of communications, unmanned satellites, missiles, computers, etc. But for two years, 1984 and 1985, some new scientific or technologically spectacular events are likely to be attempted and successfully achieved. In fact, by 1984 the US space shuttle program should be in full operation, but a much more spectacular possibility is that the USSR will establish a permanently inhabited space station with spaceships to be used for scientific, military, manufacturing, etc., purposes. During this period of time, the door is open to additional possibilities. Science today is part of many human creative activities.

To complete our investigation of event-entities, we will look at the natal planet sensitivities. For the ABG there were three events discussed that corresponded to significant peaks in the -S- graph. The table below gives the results:

Most -S- Sensitive Natal Planet(s)

	Natal Event		
Peak Event	Trinity	Hiroshima	USSR
Fusion Bomb	Sun	Moon, Saturn	Sun
Sputnik I	Venus	Mars	Venus
60-Megaton Fusion Bomb	Sun	Mars	Mars

The solar force energy is strong in the fusion bombs. As the Sun runs off fusion power, this is an appropriate result. The Moon/Saturn sensitivity for the Hiroshima chart for the fusion bomb shows an emotional connection. Moon/Saturn combinations often have to do with fears, and the development

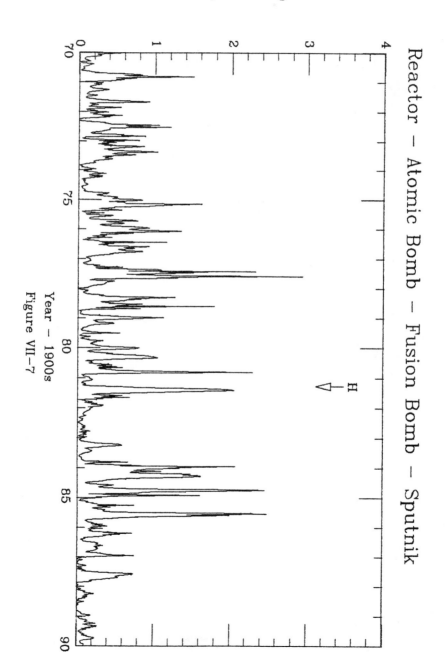

−I−

Intensity of Changes

Reactor – Atomic Bomb – Fusion Bomb – Sputnik

H

Year – 1900s

Figure VII-7

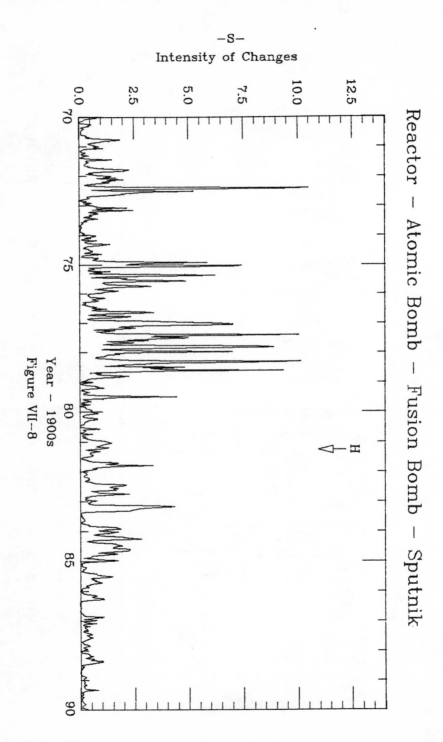

Reactor – Atomic Bomb – Fusion Bomb – Sputnik

−S−
Intensity of Changes

Year – 1900s
Figure VII–8

of the fusion bomb was a fearful event for many of those sensitive to the Hiroshima bomb.

The discussion of the *Sputnik I* natal sensitivities will be given after the next table. The 60-megaton fusion bomb natal chart sensitivities show a strong Mars component along with the Sun. The USSR devotion to larger and larger bombs went out of control with this unexpectedly large explosion. The numerous atmospheric tests during the time period near this event, by both the USSR and US, showed a devotion to the physical activity of blowing up bombs that was difficult to rationally understand. These tests were not for science, rather they were displays of military might.

The table below is for the four events used to follow the development of nuclear and space science:

Most -I- Sensitive Natal Planet(s)

Natal Event

Peak Event	Reactor	Trinity	Fusion	*Sputnik I*
Sputnik I	Mercury	Mercury, Mars	Venus	Moon
Moon Landing	Moon	Sun, Jupiter	Sun	Uranus
Space Shuttle	Uranus	Moon	Mercury	

The launching of *Sputnik I* is particularly sensitive to Venus for both -I- and -S-. There is also some sensitivity to Mercury, and satellites have revolutionized communications. The Venus sensitivity for Sputnik is indicative of the way the planet relates to scientific developments. The energies of Venus can excite not only our sensual imagination, but they can also excite the scientific imagination. Venus is also the most sensitive natal planet for the Hiroshima and USSR first atom bomb natal charts for the Sputnik event!

The landing on the Moon shows a strong Moon natal sensitivity along with a Sun sensitivity. This is a simple lesson in the elemental character of the astrological energies. If you are going to the Moon, you need Moon energies or focus of consciousness to get there. Also, a driving force is helpful, and locally the Sun is the largest astrological force or energy. The space shuttle also shows a Moon sensitivity, but Mercury and Uranus are highlighted too. The space shuttle is the first vehicle that can truly fly about in space and on Earth. It connects the human society to the future for this reason. The higher mind also does this, so the Uranus connection is appropriate. Unexpected rewards should come from the space shuttle's development.

For the four natal events listed in the second table above, there was one particular -S- event that was discussed: the Atmospheric Test Ban Treaty. In the same order as the natal events, the most sensitive -S- natal planets for this event were Saturn, Moon, Mars and Mars. Saturn brings the consequences from responsibility and is strong enough to rein in Martian devotion to physical activity. The scientific community (Saturn), the public's concern for their homes (Moon), and the military (Mars), were involved in the event.

There are certain challenges possible in human evolution, where using the explosive fires of fission and fusion are an appropriate and, in fact, necessary part of meeting the challenge. So far the world has chosen to make such a challenge for itself only once: the nuclear bombs dropped on Japan. There is nothing to say that the world must again create such a challenge. The world can learn from its first experience with the use of nuclear weapons. For the present, the world has chosen to create sufficient peace to support its scientists, artists, explorers, politicians and adventurers in business in their quest for the Moon, music, computers, biochemistry, multinational organizations and the control of fusion as one of the energy sources for the next century. And in a new step in awareness, many in the world are exploring their consciousnesses as knowledge of the tools of consciousness is becoming more available.

CHAPTER VIII

UNITED NATIONS
AND LEAGUE OF NATIONS

The League of Nations came into existence on January 10, 1920, with the signing of the Treaty of Versailles which formally ended World War I. The dream for the League was that it would evolve into an entity of sufficient political, social and commercial influence to prevent wars and promote growth or evolvement. Of course, not every nation shared in this dream.

The League succeeded as an international forum and as a sponsor of international commercial interest. But twenty years after the League's creation, the world was beginning an even greater war than the one whose ashes had been the cradle of the League's birth. The history of the League is seen in its Dynamic Astrology graphs. During the League's existence the graphs show two periods of high -S- values and one period of high -I- values. These peaks are seen in the -I- and -S- graphs (Figures VIII-1 and VIII-2) where the five events listed below are labeled:

A	09-18-1931	Japan invades Manchuria.
B	02-24-1933	Japan's ambassadors walk out of the League with the formal withdrawal on 3-27-1933.
C	12-05-1934	The first truly international force voted into existence to oversee the Saar elections.
D	09-01-1939	Germany invades Poland starting World War II.
E	06-25-1945	Vote for the UN Charter at the San Francisco conference.

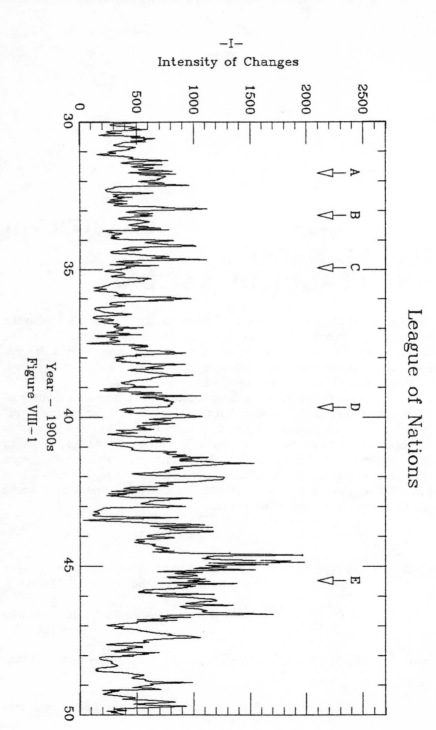

-I-
Intensity of Changes

League of Nations

Year - 1900s
Figure VIII-1

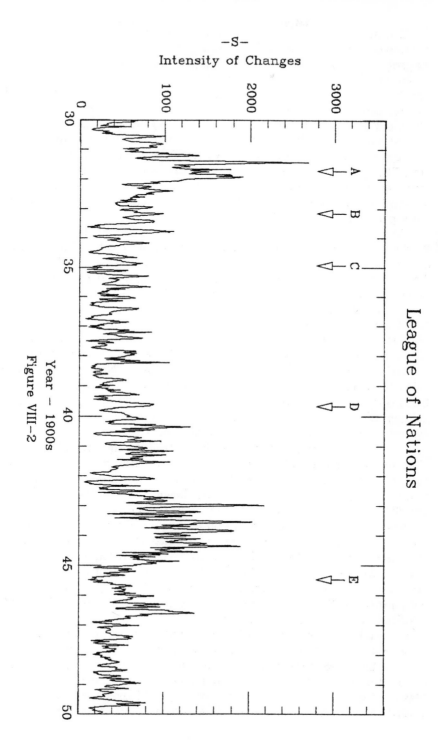

-S-
Intensity of Changes

League of Nations

Year – 1900s
Figure VIII-2

The highest -S- peak occurs in 1931, a few months before the Japanese invasion of Manchuria (event A). The League proved ineffective in handling the problem. At the same time, Hitler was coming to power in Germany. The League could do little. The next three labeled events do not correspond to significant peaks, or even peaks at all, in the -I- or -S- graphs. These events are included to show examples of activities or events related to the League which did not result in any significant change in the League. The League's big test was its handling of Japan and Germany's military activities and buildups during 1931 as well as the worldwide economic depression at the time. The US had never joined the League, and with first Japan's, and then other nations', departures from the League in the early 1930s, the League lost influence. Other entities, nations and individuals set most of the detailed timing for the events of World War II.

The second major -S- peak for the League occurs from 1943 to 1944 when World War II was at its height. Though the League was but little involved in the war as an effective force, the stress of the war is seen as the nations that had formed the League battled again. The League changed at this point in time as these nations and others looked to a future with a new world body to replace the League.

The highest -I- peak in the League's existence occurs in late 1944/early 1945 as the people and nations who had carried the League's dream in a relatively enlightened fashion strove for victory in the war. These peoples began to plan for a new League to be known as the United Nations (UN). They held conferences such as the one on banking discussed in Chapter VI. The fruits of their labors took an emotional form in 1945 when in a dramatic moment the representatives for the member nations voted (event D) for the charter of the UN at the San Francisco conference. The League had given birth.

Two events are taken for the "birth" of the UN: the vote in San Francisco and the United Nations' formal coming into existence in Washington, D.C., on October 24, 1945. Combining the graphs for these two events, the resultant -I- and -S- values for the UN are shown (Figures VIII-3 and VIII-4) for 1950-69 and (VIII-5 and VIII-6) for 1970-89. With one exception, to be discussed, the peaks in these graphs up to the present time and for the next several years are relatively low. This implies that there have been relatively few major changes in the UN since it has come into existence. This is in fact the case. Most of the changes in the UN have come about from the steady development of its various sections: UNESCO, UNICEF, etc. The UN has been involved with various peacekeeping forces in several areas of the world. Politically, however, the UN was formed to be ineffective and it remains so. Many member nations are heavily armed and in some areas frequently go to war in their attempts to tyrannize each other or "right" previous "wrongs."

The largest -S- peak in the UN graph to date, as well as a high -I- peak, occurred in early 1948 just before the nation of Israel came into being on May 15, 1948. The big power nations of the world generally supported, or at least tolerated, the formation of Israel. The Arab and several other nations did not want a Jewish national state. The rift was serious and threatened the existence of the UN as a meeting place for all of the nations of the world. However, the forces holding the UN together prevailed and the UN passed a most severe crisis. Israel and many other nations in the world came into existence shortly after World War II.

Before moving on to look at the interesting future as seen in the graphs of the UN, it is important that we look at the less major changes in the UN as they relate to the graphs for the past several decades. The events labeled in Figures VIII-3 and VIII-4 are listed below:

F	06-25-1950	Korean War begins.
G	07-27-1953	End of Korean War.
H	1958	Lebanon crisis of 1958.
I	07-14-1960	UN forces go into the Congo.
J	10-1962	Cuban missile crisis.
	12-1962	Major UN military actions in the Congo.
K	06-30-1964	UN forces leave Congo.

Two -S- peaks of equal height are seen during this time period (Figure VIII-4). On the first -S- peak, the UN was heavily involved in the Korean War which had started at event F. On the highest -I- peak (event G), the UN-sponsored negotiations to end the Korean war succeeded (Figure VIII-3). Note that the -S- value is quite low at this time.

The UN -I- and -S- levels were very low in 1956 when the USSR crushed a rebellion in Hungary, and the Arabs and Israelis had a period of fighting intense enough to change borders for a short time. The UN sent some peacekeeping forces into the Mideast after the war, but otherwise there was only talk or resolutions for both the Hungarian and Mideast situations. The UN was unprepared or unable to function effectively in these situations and did not change enough to deal with them. However, the -I- and -S- levels were up in 1958 during the Lebanon crisis. The UN sent observers into the area, but they failed in their task of finding out what was causing the violence in the country. The US then sent troops into the area to stop the civil war and Syrian activities. The UN grew with this event via having made an attempt to do something effective even though the results were nil.

The second major -S- peak in this time period relates to two situations. The UN presence in the Congo had started at event I (a few months from a narrow -I- peak). The UN military actions in the Congo climaxed at the height of the second major -S- peak (event J). The second stressful situation

-I-

Intensity of Changes

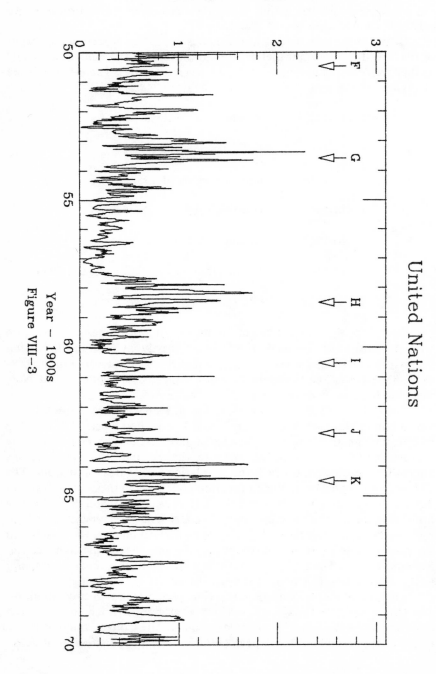

United Nations

Year — 1900s
Figure VIII-3

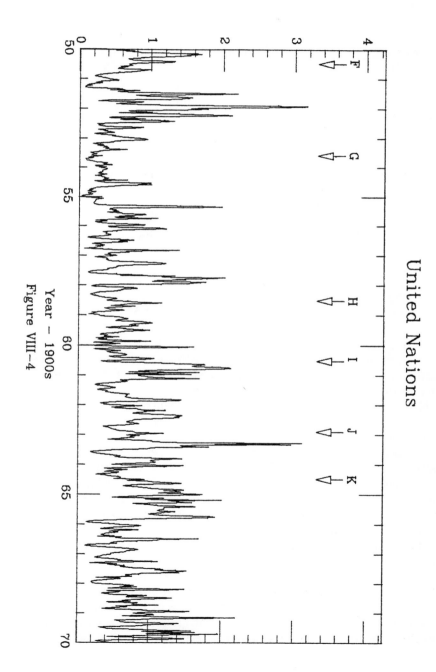

−S−
Intensity of Changes

United Nations

Year − 1900s
Figure VIII−4

was the Cuban missile crisis which occurred at almost the same time. The US and USSR were toying with each other. In response, the UN and the world shuddered, prayed and grew up a little. The UN forces withdrew from the Congo (event K) as the -I- values peaked and interestingly, the situation between the US and USSR improved shortly thereafter. The US received new leadership in late 1963 and the USSR in late 1964. This point of view does not excuse the assassination of US President Kennedy, but the fact remains that most of the world did not want to be turned into radioactive dust and preferred leaders who could find less endangering toys to work out their problems.

The UN -I- and -S- values were low in the late 1960s as the US and others tried to destroy much of Vietnam via one method or another. When the big powers play(ed), the UN members talk(ed). The Arabs and Israelis carried out another one of their border adjustments via warfare.

Moving to the next two decades, the two highest -I- peaks are found since the formation of the UN. The -I- and -S- graphs for this time period are shown (Figures VIII-5 and VIII-6) and the labeled events are listed below:

L	09-25-1971	The People's Republic of China (PRC) is admitted to the UN.
M	12-13-1972	The US achieves a favorable vote in the General Assembly to reduce its share of expenditures from 31.5% to 25%.

With event L, the PRC became a member of the UN. It also took its permanent seat on the Security Council. With event M, the US achieved a significant step in making the world as a whole more responsible for the activities of the UN. Both of these moves were critical developments for the UN if it was or is to truly have worldwide validity.

A medium level of stressful change is also observed at the time of event M and for several years afterward. The UN was involved with problems in the Mideast and problems of terrorism and colonialism. The UN was slowly growing and changing as it tried to meet some of the challenges in the world.

When permanent members of the UN Security Council are involved in armed or serious political conflict with nonpermanent members, we usually do not see the UN changing enough to get effectively involved. The USSR incursions into Hungary and Afghanistan, the US incursion into Vietnam and the Great Britain/Argentina war over the Falkland Islands are a few examples of this. The permanent members have been too powerful for the UN to have a major effect in these situations. When the permanent members are in conflict with each other, we do observe some changes or more effective actions taken by the UN. Examples are US/USSR confrontations in Korea and Cuba. The UN has served as a meeting ground for the powerful parties involved. The UN has also been a more effective force in its military/political involvements with the less powerful nations of the world when they have difficulties with each other. The UN is a powerful force relative to many of these less powerful nations.

The UN and the world are in a situation now similar to the states in America during the time period after the Revolutionary War and before the US Constitution. None of the states wanted to give up its sovereignty to a larger governmental body, but the overall forces of security, economics, culture and centralized political power were in the direction of a central government. The difference between this analogy and the world today is that the American states had a more homogeneous culture and tended to be less violent with each other at the time of the US achieving independence than some of the nations of the world are today.

Philosophically and politically speaking, the challenge is the age-old one of the individual's freedom versus the group's needs. The point of balance that arises from meeting this challenge is always in motion. The direction of motion is determined by the choices of the individuals, the groups that they form, and the environment in space and time in which they have chosen to reside. The point of balance for the UN will soon move significantly.

Look now to where the -I- and -S- graphs for the UN are shown for the present time period (Figures VII-5 and VII-6). In the spring of 1989 there is an -S- peak far higher than any previous -S- peak in the history of the UN and at that time the -I- values are low. The UN has fulfilled much of the dream that went into its formation and the formation of the League, except in the areas of being a significant political power. The year the UN will change politically is 1989. Due to the changes in the world occurring in 1984, 1988 and early 1989, discussed in the chapter on World Powers, the UN will be in a position to either become an institution of political power or drop like the League from the center of world attention and activity. Physical world events, the peoples and nations of the world and the leaders of the time will determine where the place of the UN will be in the balance of the political, social, economic and cultural fabric of the world.

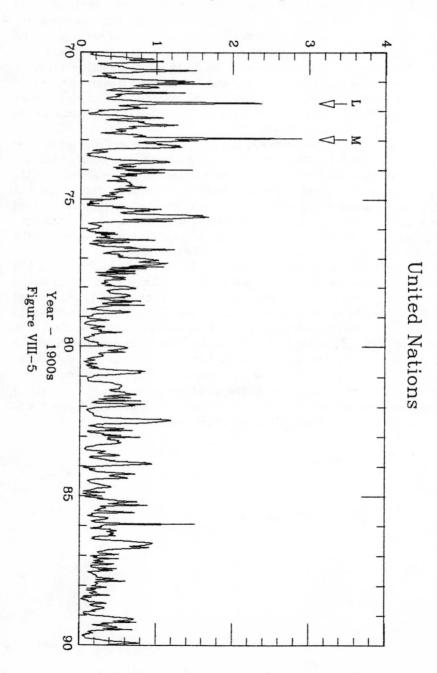

−I−
Intensity of Changes

United Nations

Year – 1900s
Figure VIII–5

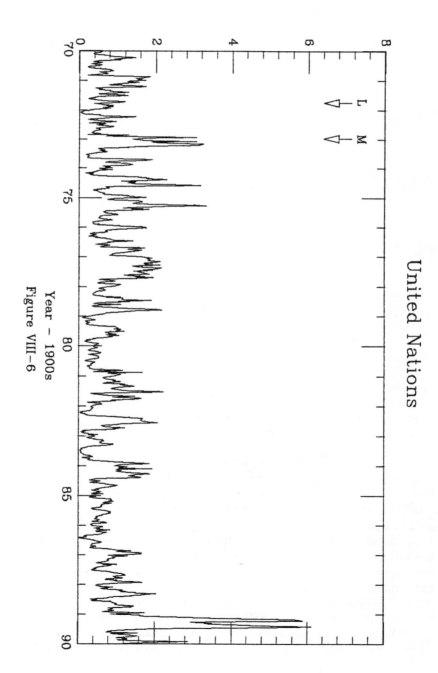

−S−
Intensity of Changes

United Nations

Year − 1900s
Figure VIII−6

CHAPTER IX
WORLD POWERS

Due to the complexity of the issues involved, this chapter is divided into four sections:

Section I:	Astrology of the 1980s
Section II:	Political Trends for the 1980s
Section III:	The Sequence of Events
Section IV:	Individuals and World Events

In this chapter the word "political" will be used in its broadest sense. Treat the usage of this word to include the spectrum of social, economic, cultural and even religious events associated with the upcoming world changes.

Section I: Astrology of the 1980s

There are three astrological events of particular note occurring during the 1980s. The first of these events occurs in late 1983 and early 1984 when Pluto enters the astrological sign of Scorpio and, more importantly, Jupiter is exactly conjunct Neptune as they enter the sign of Capricorn. This latter event has to do with commerce, and in particular, oil-related commerce. If we look at all of the -I- and -S- graphs shown in this book for that time period, the only group that has high -I- and -S- peaks in late 1983 or 1984 for all of its members is the group of economic entities that is discussed in Chapter VI, World Banking. Note that some of the graphs in Chapter IV show medium peaks at this time and the USSR shows a very high -S- peak.

Whether consciously chosen or not, the births of the IMF, EEC and OPEC were timed so as to make use of this astrological event for major changes. Noting that J. P. Morgan used Evangeline Adams as his astrologer, it may be that astrologically knowledgeable leaders of commerce were involved in setting up these institutions of commerce. Another viable explanation is that at the sub- or superconscious level the groups involved clairvoyantly saw the 1984 astrological event and adjusted the nativity of their related institutions to maximally make use of the event. Recall from the chapter on Nuclear Energy and Space the connectedness of the nativities, and most scientists do not use astrology consciously at this time.

The second astrological event of note is that Saturn and Uranus repeat Jupiter's and Neptune's act in February 1988 by also being exactly conjunct as they enter the sign of Capricorn. However, except for some of the Mideast countries and the IMF's -S- graph, early 1988 does not appear to be a time of high -I- or -S- peaks. This result came as a surprise to me. I had expected this event to be more generally significant in the political graphs. Since we do not observe many changes predicted with the -I- or -S- graphs, we can use more conventional astrological analyses to see the character of this event. The Saturn (responsibility)/Uranus (higher mind, the unexpected) conjunction on the cusp of Capricorn (Shiva, Christmas, winter solstice) denotes changes in the weather and can indicate unexpected losses and gifts to many individuals. In Hindu terminology many payments of *karma* will come due and be collected. Politically, the Mideast will see major changes.

The third astrological event of note is related to the world's political powers and is the conjunction (to one degree) of Saturn and Neptune taking place while in opposition to the star Sirius in the spring of 1989. Numerous graphs shown in this book show -S- peaks in the spring of 1989. The details will be discussed in Section III of this chapter. As for the event, until now stars have not been discussed in this book and stars are not included in the Dynamic Astrology computations. Saturn and Neptune are conjunct approximately every 47 years so it is not their conjunction *per se* that is critical in making this event of particular note. Sirius is the brightest star in the sky and it is also a double star. The smaller of the two stars is a white dwarf. Almost every ancient culture worked with the energies of Sirius via temples, calendars and even cities set to align with its position. Many political systems have been tied to Sirius, because its energies can be used in setting up leader-follower relationships as well as promoting spiritual evolution. The Saturn/Neptune conjunction in opposition to Sirius indicates an upcoming focus on these ties and relationships: perhaps by breaking some of the old ones, facilitating the modification of existing ones and being used for the creation of new ones.

Section II: Political trends for the 1980s

The world is about to take a major step in its evolvement. To see this, consider the example of Europe. There was a time when the provinces and cities of France warred with each other and similarly in England, Germany, etc.

Occasionally a leader such as Charlemagne, or a venture such as the Crusades, or the much earlier Roman invasion, would unify a larger region. As communications, transportation and the general level of education increased in Europe, the size of the political units increased. Wars were carried out at the level of England versus France, etc.

World Wars I and II climaxed and transcended centuries of European warfare at the level of nation versus nation(s). In western Europe today there is no inclination for England, France, Italy, Spain, West Germany, etc., to go to war with each other. Instead, these nations have joined with each other in forming significant multinational institutions for trade, military and political activities. A similar process has occurred in eastern Europe. Today the border of contention is between the multinational groups of eastern and western Europe as well as other multinational organizations.

Since World War II, worldwide instant communications and computer networks have been achieved as well as a greatly increased ability to transport goods. Due to the related rapid development of science and technology in the world, the immediate challenges are no longer technical but political. The question before the world is whether to go through a new wave of warfare as a step to forming a world political system, or whether the nations and groups of nations of the world will nonviolently sacrifice some of their hallowed beliefs so as to provide a viable world political system.

The idea of an effective world government is repulsive to many individuals and nations today. But for centuries the direction of motion in political systems has been for larger political units. In most but not all cases, the larger political units have proved beneficial to the populations involved. Consider the following list of reasonable world goals that are often mentioned by the current leaders in the world:

> Stabilized and equitable commodity prices
> Disarmament
> End of dangerous drug trade
> Reduction of pollution
> Stabilized populations

Imagine how many people's livelihoods would have to change to even attempt achieving these goals, disregarding the fact that there are many who would not want these goals. For example, one of the main functions of religion is to regulate sexual behavior. What will religions do if stabilized populations are achieved? Further, would having a world government help with achieving these goals?

Until the satellite communication and computer networks were installed, an effective world government was not possible. During the past decade these networks have been installed and they are rapidly expanding. A world government is now possible.

Section III: The Sequence of Events

Economically, the world today is a closely interconnected place. In 1984 these interconnections, the money exchange rates and the world banking system will be significantly altered. The detailed discussion is given in Chapter VI, World Banking. A new, more fully computerized system may be installed in its place. The new system will not operate under some of the more faulty current assumptions, e.g., that every nation can have a net surplus in their balance of payments. It will be some time after 1984 before international commerce returns to its current level. However, some nations will quickly prosper with the new system.

The USSR, US and western Europe will put forth rescue plans for the floundering nations of the world. In 1986 due to the changes discussed in Chapter VI and the level of stress shown between the USSR and US (Figure IX-1), there is hope that they might accomplish some of their goals. Remember, some of the great leaders have launched their projects in stressful situations in the past (see Chapters II and IV). The question will be whether in 1986 Europe, the USSR and US jointly solve the external stressful problems or treat each other as the problem. The quality of the leaders in power at the time will be the key to the directions taken. Note that the quality of the leaders depends on the character of the populations they lead. The situation is not circular; rather, as seen in time, it is a spiral.

Figure IX-2 gives the combined -I- values for the "Big Three" world political powers (the PRC, USSR and US). We see that the decade of the 1970s was a time of cooperation and initiative. What is important is that the Big Three have had experience with some cooperation. Even though there may be stressful times in the future, the practiced patterns of cooperation can still be used. There are powerful forces for evolution via peaceful means available in the world.

With their bank accounts low or empty, the Mideast will see major changes during 1987, if not sooner. Both Group 1 and 2 nations (Chapter V, the Mideast) in the Mideast show significant stress in 1987 (Figures V-4 and V-8). Although there are individual exceptions, the oil-producing (Group 1) nations do not as a group show stress after 1987. Israel's neighbors (the Group 2 nations) do show stress after 1987 with the level cycling to its highest value in the two decades during the spring of 1989. All of these nations have been addicted to the easy oil money. Their withdrawal symptoms at its loss or reduced supply are likely to be unpleasant.

The Big Three's combined -S- graph is shown in Figure IX-3. There is only one peak: the spring of 1989! The UN's high -S- level is in the spring of 1989. Its implications are discussed in detail in Chapter VIII. The Mideast (Figure V-8), Canada (Figure II-14), India (Figure IV-8) and West Germany all have high -S- peaks in the spring of 1989. All of these political units will have stressful changes on the Saturn/Neptune conjunction in opposition to Sirius in the spring of 1989.

The sequence of events is that the economic changes, set in motion in

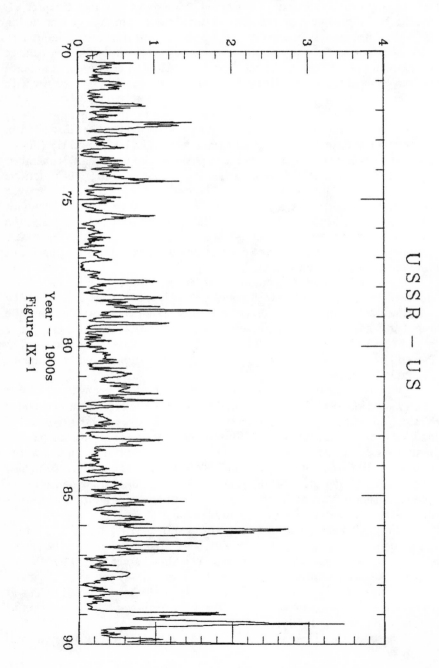

-S-
Intensity of Changes

USSR - US

Year - 1900s
Figure IX-1

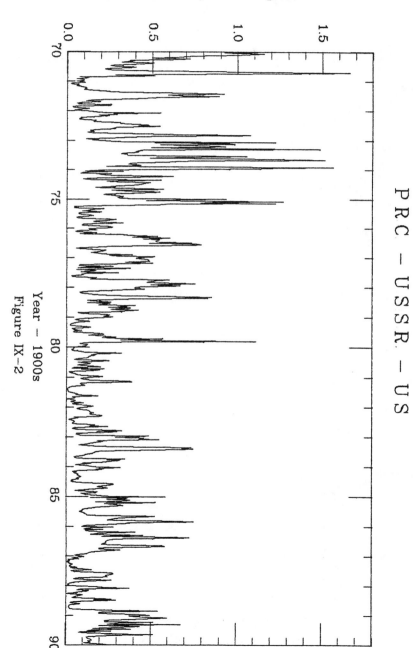

-I-
Intensity of Changes

PRC – USSR – US

Year – 1900s
Figure IX-2

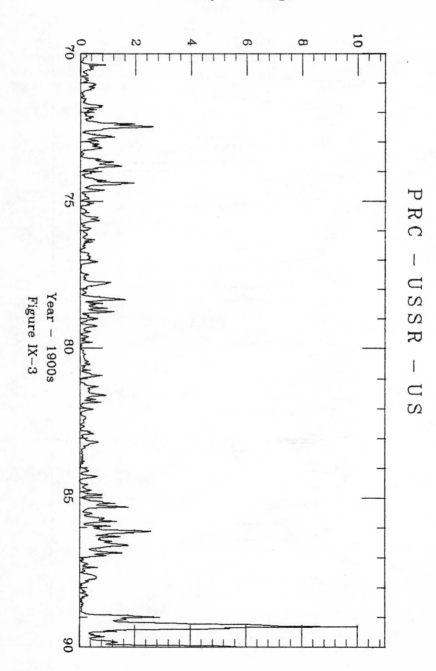

-S-
Intensity of Changes

PRC - USSR - US

Year - 1900s

Figure IX-3

1984, will result in political changes. The pattern will be that economic disasters such as Mexico (Figure II-17) and India (Figure IV-8) will be the first to effect political change. There will be significant political changes in the USSR at this time (Figure IV-4). Then the Mideast will begin changing politically. In the spring of 1989 the world as a whole will face a great challenge. Humanity may generate the surrounding events from the activity of its politics or nature may take the projected mental and emotional thought forms of humanity, add the astrological energies discussed above and create a world-scale "natural" event. In either case, those forces pushing for a world government will take these key points in time to act to achieve their goals.

I have indicated the astrology of the 1980s with conventional analyses that might only be believed by astrologers and I have indicated the astrology of the 1980s with Dynamic Astrology results that, due to this book, might be more generally believed. I have indicated the political trends in the world for the past several millennia. But we have free will, so the "what" is not yet determined, especially in detail. However, having chosen to incarnate as citizens of human nations at this point in time and space, the "when" is largely determined. The "when" for the world as a whole is 1984 and the spring of 1989.

Section IV: Individuals and World Events

Every year, somewhere on the Earth there is a birth, a death, a healing, a harvest, a marriage, an enchanted evening, a bit of war, an earthquake, an active religious leader, an active spiritual leader and, according to some, a UFO landing. So whatever you think 1984 and 1989 will bring, if you can't wait and you want it enough, you can get most of it within a year someplace on Earth. From the point of view of an individual, 1984 and 1989 will not be very different from any other year.

Yet the lives of many individuals will have major changes in 1984 and 1989 because so many individuals have their lives tied to the nations and states in which they live. Depending on how the events go, the tendency for individuals to tie their lives to nations and/or world governments may be enhanced or decreased. Evolvement occurs in either case. From these activities, both individuals and groups of individuals gain experience and greater awareness.

The years 1984 and 1989 will also herald a new period of great world leaders. The events that begin at these times will, of course, take some time to come to fruition. There will be a variety of movements and leaders to watch, join or avoid, depending on individual taste. One implication is that many of those individuals who will become the new, world-class leaders have already incarnated and are living on Earth.

Evolvement means in part that you can gain awareness of when, where and why you made the choices that have brought you to the point in the world at which you now find yourself. And by extension, evolvement means that you can gain awareness of how to take yourself to any other place in the drama of the world that you choose. *Karma* means that whether you like to or not, you take responsibility for your actions along what ever path you have chosen. When you are evolved enough to see or know and love your *karma*, you are without fear. Nineteen eighty-four and nineteen eighty-nine will be years like all other years: years of evolvement and *karma*, and years of fearless, creative, loving and inspirational possibilities, if you so choose. The world will go on after 1989, even though the graphs in this book do not. I have calculated many of the graphs for the next several decades and the results are intriguing to say the least. I recommend them to you.

Chapter X

CONCLUSIONS

In the first chapter, Dynamic Astrology's Development, I posed several questions. The examples presented in the subsequent chapters represent detailed responses to these questions. In summary, the graphs present astrological information in a symbol system easily understandable by the educated public. The concept of the scale of the intensity of changes is clear and examples of the use of this scale over centuries have been presented. Results for groups of entities have also been presented that show not only when their major changes will occur but also give a relative measure of these groups' connectedness. Entities that are people, countries and even events have been studied. But something more also happened in the evolution of this book. As I studied the examples, I discovered that at two points in time in the near future, large-scale world changes are predicted.

If no major world changes had been discovered for the near future, this book would have been just an intellectual curiosity for the observing astrologer. Or more likely, I would not have been inclined to do the work for this book. Solutions and events match their times as has been repeatedly observed in this book. Astrology is already a tool of statecraft in many nations of the world. With the results presented in this book, astrology and its tools, such as Dynamic Astrology, will be used by even greater numbers of the people of the world.

To evolve, we become aware. With awareness, one thing we discover about the world is that astrology plays a part in it. In recent centuries, and particularly the last one, science has been used to expand our awareness. Science will continue to serve this function. It needs, however, to be stated that the results presented in this book utilize astrology which is an art and not a science. It may be that some day, when consciousness and its possible connection to the quantum mechanics and theories of measurement are understood, the link between science and astrology will be made or that some other link may be chosen for demonstration. For now I repeat, that the results presented in this book are astrological and I add that they are valid.

Dynamic Astrology is a quantum step beyond conventional astrology and yet it is consistent with conventional astrology. As the tools for the astrologers improve, so will the opportunities to practice their art. As it has been in the past and is now in some places in the present, the astrological view of the world can be one of the guiding lights of the future.

NATAL INFORMATION

All of the natal information used as input for the computation of the -I- and -S- Dynamic Astrology graphs presented in this book is given in this appendix. For simplicity of presentation, it is assumed that the reader of this appendix is familiar with basic astrology and algebra. Recall that these assumptions were not made for the chapters of this book. Following the discussion of the basic concepts of natal information, the detailed natal information will be given in a sequence corresponding to that of the chapters. Within each chapter the pattern will be to present the natal information of the people first, then the countries, institutions and events. The only exceptions to this pattern of presentation will be several examples given initially to help with the explanation of the use of Dynamic Astrology in working with natal information.

The first concept in working with natal information is to know what correct natal information is. The second concept is to get accurate historical information. The third concept is to be very careful with anything you do beyond exercising the first two concepts. You will notice that for this book most of the natal information used in calculating the graphs has not involved going beyond using the first two concepts, except that the "nativity at noon" idea, discussed below, is used for some nativities. However, very interesting Dynamic Astrology concepts are presented in this appendix on some new ways in going beyond the first two concepts and even verifying some of the first and second concept information.

The concept of the correct natal information of a human being is simple. The instant when a newborn infant's first breath is taken is the moment of birth. Many other events also have clear or obvious instants of birth. The moments that the first laser, transistor and controlled fission reaction went into operation are examples. The launching of a satellite is less obvious as there are two times: the moment of launch and the moment of going into operation. Fortunately with Dynamic Astrology, handling entities with multiple birth times is relatively easy.

For the examples given so far, there are clear moments of birth and the angles can clearly be used. When we come to the birth of a country or institution, the idea of a moment of birth is not as obvious. However, to give two examples, some countries — such as Canada — and some institutions — such as the League of Nations — had clearly stated moments of birth accurate to a minute or two. Other countries such as Lebanon had a day of events during the course of which they have achieved their independence. If a country or institution had a clear moment of birth, I included the angles in the graphs. If the country had a birth that lasted over the course of a day, then I used local noon for the time of birth. If the country had a birth taking place over a several-hour period, then I used the end of that period for the time of birth. For these last two cases the angles were not included in the calculations, but the Moon and other planets were included for the natal and progressed planets.

One additional class of entities has also been used for examples in this book: meetings that serve as the births of entities. Some examples are the Bretton Woods meeting that set up the IMF, the San Francisco meeting that set up the UN, and the meeting of the Continental Congress that resulted in the US Declaration of Independence. The correct moment of birth for the entities that sprang from these meetings is not the start of the meeting, nor the public announcement of the results of the meeting, nor necessarily the formal end of the meeting. The correct moment is either the moment of voting, or the end of the signing of documents, or other decision-making process whereby those present made a clear declaration of support for the entity whose birth was taking place. The examples to be given in this appendix provide further details on this first concept: correct natal information.

The natal information will be presented in the following format:

Name of Entity   Reference No.
MO-DAY-YEAR, UT (HH:MM:SS)
Longitude, Latitude

Where UT is Universal (Greenwich) Time
    HH is hours
    MM is minutes
    SS is seconds (when available)

The longitude and latitude are given only if the natal angles have been included in the calculations of -I- and or -S- values. The references are listed at the end of this appendix.

The second concept, accurate historical information, seems simple enough, except that accurate historical information is not always available. For example, in the case of the signing of the Declaration of Independence of the US, there is conflicting historical information as to the time of day of the signing. My solution to this question of accuracy in all cases, including the birth of the US has been to make the best choice based on my analyses of available information and give appropriate references.

Fortunately, with astrology the issue of accuracy can be dealt with in a straightforward manner. If an entity's moment of birth is known to within a minute or two, we can use the angles. If an entity's moment of birth is known to within a few hours, we can use the Moon. If an entity's birth is known to a day, we can leave out the natal Moon but use the Sun and planets. These statements apply to Dynamic Astrology. In conventional astrology some questions related to the angles can be dealt with using larger uncertainties in the natal times.

Leaving out the natal Moon is not desirable, even if the birth is known only to the accuracy of having occurred on one day. The choice of what to do moves us into the third concept of natal information: methods of improving on the historical natal information. The first method I call the "nativity of noon," where local noon is used for the time of birth. The Moon is included, but not the angles in the calculations. This method works very well and is used in this book. Whenever in the examples "noon" is listed after the UT, this method has been used. Note that the times have been rounded off to the nearest hour as well. It is worth discussing for a moment why this method works. Many of the fields of energy or consciousness associated with astrology have focal points at sunrise, noon, sunset or midnight. Consciousness and energy-related rituals frequently are set to take place at one of these times. I have usually chosen the noon focal point because in the majority of cases the birthing events have spanned most of a day. The focal point of noon is not as strong as the actual time of birth if that time is different from noon, but it is strong enough to be used as the time of birth if more accurate information is not available.

To go beyond the "nativity at noon" method, we can use Dynamic Astrology to provide us with a new and powerful tool for verifying and improving on natal information. I have used this new tool on the natal information of several of the entities used as examples in the chapters of this book. Wherever I have done this, a detailed discussion is provided in this appendix so that the reader can observe the use of this tool. First, a detailed discussion of the tool is required. For an entity the -I- or -S- values can be thought of as functions of two time variables: the time of the nativity, **TN**, and the time of the event, **TE**. This can be expressed algebraically as:

$$\text{-I-} = \text{-I-} (TN, TE)$$
and
$$\text{-S-} = \text{-S-} (TN, TE)$$

In calculating all of the graphs shown in the chapters, TN has been fixed for each entity and TE has been varied over a span of twenty years.

To investigate the natal time for an entity, we can choose an event in the entity's life that was a major change for the entity, fix TE and vary TN to see if -I- and/or -S- has a peak at the believed value of TN. This works, but it can be made much better if many events corresponding to major changes for the entity are used as well as multiple -I- and -S- values at the same time. The generalized concept is to calculate a new function called the Natal Intensity Function, **-N-** , for a variety of events, **TE1, TE2,** etc. using both -I- and -S assignments as appropriate. The equation for **-N-** is:

$$\text{-N-} = \text{-N-(TN)} = C * \overset{mj}{\underset{j=1}{P}} \text{-I-(TN, TEj)} * \overset{mk}{\underset{k=1}{P}} \text{-S-(TN, TEk)}$$

* \quad means multiply
P \quad means take the product of
j \quad is the number of any -I- event
k \quad is the number of any -S- event
mj \quad is the total number of -I- events
mk \quad is the total number of -S- events
C \quad is an arbitrary constant used to facilitate plotting the -N- values on some reasonable scale. We are more interested in the variation of -N- with TN than its absolute magnitude.

The values of -N- are clearly influenced by the events chosen. The examples will serve to help the reader be sensitive to this issue. -N- will vary rapidly for changes in TN of only a minute or two if the natal angles are included in calculating the -I- and -S- values. If the natal angles are not included, then -N- will vary for changes in TN on the order of an hour or two.

The values of -N- are also dependent on the orb parameter, W, discussed in Appendix B, and the choice of transiting planets used in the calculation. In the chapters, W was always taken as 1.0, but it is interesting to investigate the value of 0.5 for some of the examples of using -N-. The transiting planets in the chapters were always Jupiter through Pluto plus the nodes of the Moon, which corresponds to the label in the graphs of Trans = (10,14). For the examples of -N- it will be occasionally interesting to use Trans = (6,14), which means the Sun through Pluto but not the Moon. For the Trans = (6,14) the UT of the events must be known to a few hours, but for the Trans = (10,14) the events must be known only to an accuracy of a day, or sometimes several days depending on how fast Jupiter and Saturn are moving at the time of the event.

In the examples where -N- is calculated, the W and Trans values are 1.0 and (10,14) unless otherwise stated. In the graphs of -N-, note that TN is given as UT in decimal hours.

If -N- has been calculated, then it is always discussed and the events that have been used are listed as:

-I- , -S- or -*-, MO-DAY-YEAR, UT

UT is included only if a tran = (6,14) has been used. -*- means that the event is taken twice, once as -I-, and once as -S-. A graph of -N- values will sometimes be given as well.

The first example of using -N- values will be the League of Nations.

League of Nations   Ref. 1
01-10-1920, 16:19
2E07, 48N48

The League of Nations came into being with the signing of the Treaty of Versailles. The ceremony took place between 4:17 and 4:20 PM at the Palace of Versailles on the date given above. Premier Clemenceau of France stated ". . . from this moment the treaty enters into effect . . ." (Ref. 1). -N- has been calculated for the League using the following events:

-*-,	09-08-1926,	12	Vote to bring Germany into the League.
-S-,	09-18-1931,	12	Invasion of Manchuria by Japan.
-S-,	02-24-1933,	12	Japanese walk out of the League.
-S-,	10-14-1933,	12	Hitler announces German withdrawal.
-I-,	12-05-1934,	12	Formation of Saar peacekeeping force.
-S-,	09-01-1939,	5	Start of World War II.
-I-,	06-26-1945,	30	San Francisco conference vote on UN.
-I-,	10-24-1945,	17	Opening of UN.

The -N- values for two choices of W and Tran are given in Figure A-1. The -N- values have been normalized to one for the highest values shown. For both choices of W and Tran, the peak is at UT = 16.31 hours which is 4:19 PM. The conclusion by both historically recorded information and Dynamic Astrology -N- values is that the League of Nations had a birth which took place in a time of a few minutes or less.

There are some additional observations about the -N- values for the League that are important. If UTs beyond the range shown in the figure are used then there are -N- values higher than the one at UT = 16.31. However, the historical information limits the range we need to scan to the times shown in the figure or less. If random sets of dates covering the life of the League are used for the event times, then, in general, a peak is not observed at 16.31 or near it. It is important to check the -N- values with random dates because even with random dates, -N- will show some systematic structure.

The final observation for the -N- graph of the League is that the Ascendant is sextile the Moon and semi-sextile Mars and the Vertex is conjunct Venus, all to within one degree. It is possible that what has been determined is a sensitivity to these natal planets. However, this sensitivity does not in general show up as peaks in -N- for every point where the angles make these or other aspects that are multiples of thirty degrees to these planets. In

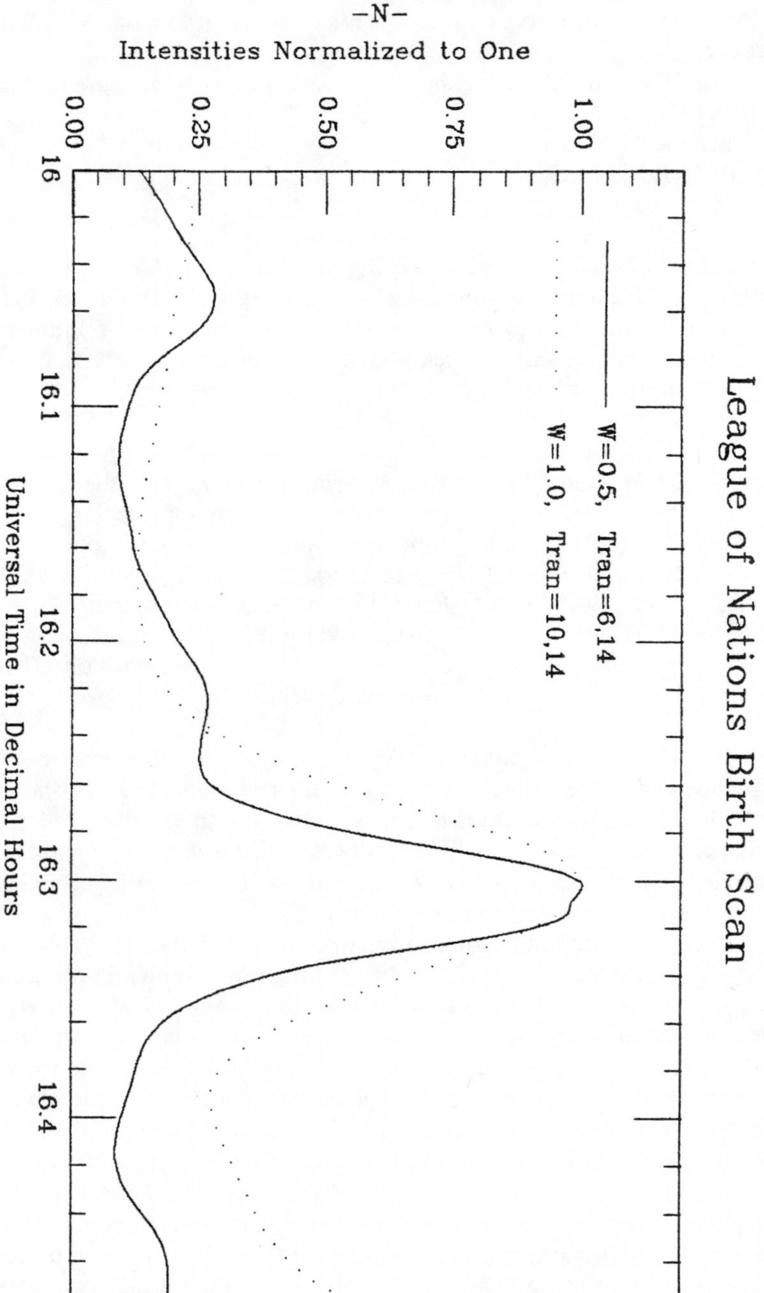
League of Nations Birth Scan
W=0.5, Tran=6,14
W=1.0, Tran=10,14
-N-
Intensities Normalized to One
0.00
0.25
0.50
0.75
1.00
16
16.1
16.2
16.3
16.4
16.5
Universal Time in Decimal Hours

Figure A-1

studying -N- graphs, natal planet sensitivities are always seen. The calculation of -N- for the League has been done in detail so that the reader can see some of the beauty of the concepts as well as some of the problems that can arise. -N- must be used like any complex tool, with care and practice before conclusions can be drawn.

Our next examples of using -N- are the three entities that were used as the first example of the use of Dynamic Astrology in this book: Benjamin Franklin, Thomas Jefferson and George Washington. Benjamin Franklin was born in a house next to the Old South Church in Boston and baptized on the day of his birth. We would not expect him to be born late in the day or the evening.

Benjamin Franklin   Ref. 2, 3, 4
01-17-1706, 06:30

-N- values have been calculated for Franklin using the following events in his life:

-*-,	08-18-1721	First issue of newspaper with brother
-*-,	10-03-1723	Arrival in Philadelphia
-*-,	01-04-1725	Arrival in London, England
-*-,	10-13-1729	First issue of newspaper in Philadelphia
-*-,	09-12-1730	Marriage to Deborah
-*-,	12-30-1732	First *Poor Richard's Almanac*
-*-,	07-27-1757	Arrival in London as colonial representative
-*-,	07-04-1776	Birth of US
-*-,	09-17-1787	Signing of US Constitution
-*-,	04-17-1790	Death

The -N- values are shown in Figure A-2. The highest point is at a UT = 6.5 hours which corresponds to approximately 1:30 AM local time. This time is consistent with historical facts.

Thomas Jefferson's birth time is known only to the day. The following events have been used in calculating -N- values for his day of birth:

-*-,	08-17-1757	Death of father
-*-,	01-01-1772	Marriage to Martha
-*-,	07-04-1776	Birth of US
-*-,	06-01-1779	Governor of Virginia
-*-,	08-06-1784	Arrival in Paris
-*-,	09-17-1787	Signing of US Constitution
-*-,	03-04-1801	Becomes US President
-*-,	07-04-1826	Death

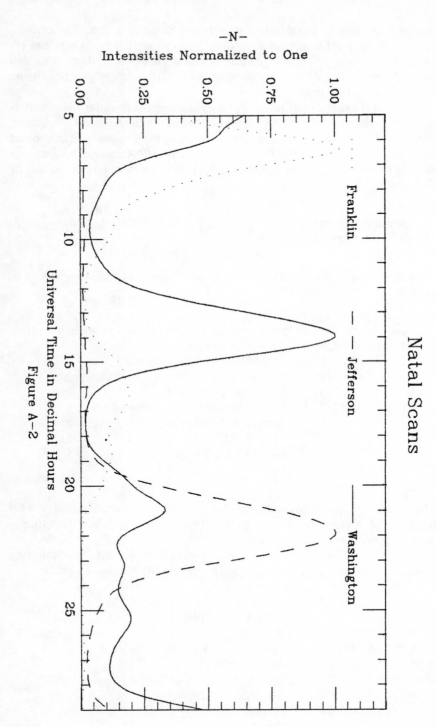

Figure A-2

Jefferson's -N- values are shown in Figure A-2. There is a single peak at a UT = 22, 5:00 PM local time.

Thomas Jefferson   Ref. 5
04-13-1743, 22:00

George Washington's birth is historically recorded to have occurred at 10:00 AM.

George Washington   Ref. 6
02-22-1732, 15:00

It is interesting to calculate -N- values for him to see if we see the expected peak at UT = 15. The events used are:

-*-,	05-28-1754	First military attack in French and Indian War
-*-,	01-06-1759	Marriage to Martha
-*-,	06-15-1775	Commander of Colonial Army
-*-,	07-04-1776	Birth of US
-*-,	09-17-1787	Signing of US Constitution
-*-,	04-30-1789	Becomes first US President
-*-,	12-14-1799	Death

Washington's -N- values are shown in Figure A-2. The largest peak is at UT = 14. The full width at half maximum of the peak is two hours and the accuracy of recording births at Washington's time was typically a quarter to a half hour. The conclusion is that the -N- values for Washington are consistent with the historically recorded information.

Having used -N- values to adjust the hour of birth for two of these three individuals, a question arises as to how much Figures II-1 and II-2 were affected by this. To investigate this question, the following procedure was used. A new set of -N- values was determined for all three individuals using only the event of -I-, 9-17-1787. Then a second set of -N- values was determined using only the event of -S-, 7-4-1776. For Franklin, new values of UT were determined for before 6:00 PM for the lowest value of -N-. For Jefferson, the new UTs were determined for the lowest values of -N- for the whole day. For Washington, the new UTs were determined for the lowest values of -N- for a four-hour period centered around the recorded time of his birth. The resulting new natal times are listed below:

Event: -I-, 9-17-1787 — Signing of Constitution.
Franklin	UT = 10:30	Natal Inputs
Jefferson	UT = 12:00	for
Washington	UT = 16:00	Figure A-3

Event: -S-, 7-4-1776 — Declaration of Independence.
Franklin	UT = 08:00	Natal Inputs
Jefferson	UT = 06:30	for
Washington	UT = 14:00	Figure A-4

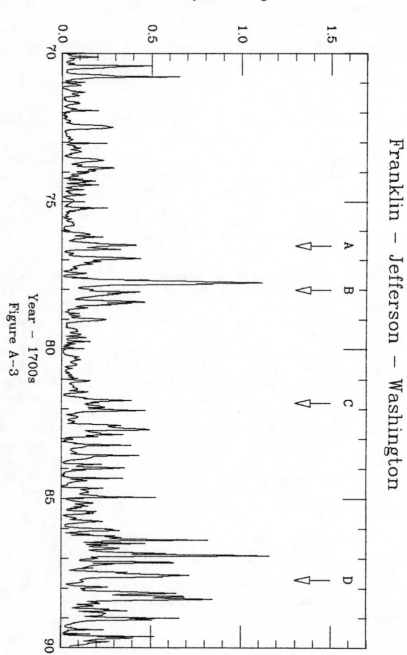

−I−
Intensity of Changes

Franklin − Jefferson − Washington

Year − 1700s

Figure A−3

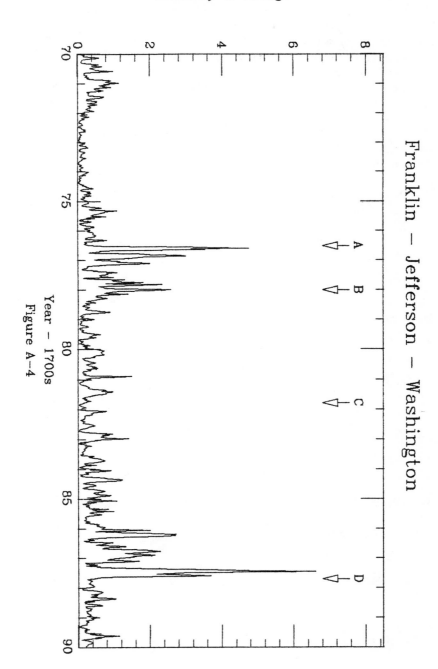

-S-
Intensity of Changes

Franklin — Jefferson — Washington

Year — 1700s

Figure A-4

Using these new natal times new -I- and -S- combined graphs were then calculated for these three individuals. The results are shown in Figures A-3 and A-4 for the above sets as indicated and are to be compared to Figures II-1 and II-2 respectively. The -I- peaks in 1777 and 1786 are slightly reduced. The -S- peaks corresponding to the signing of the Declaration of Independence and Constitution are higher. Having the correct information in clearly important, but for the major peaks, being close to the correct time usually gives the significant results.

Chapter by chapter, the natal information is given below for all of the graphs.

Chapter II — Natal Information

Benjamin Franklin (given in the introduction to this appendix)
Thomas Jefferson (given in the introduction to this appendix)

Abraham Lincoln   Ref. 7
02-12-1809, 13:00

Richard M. Nixon   Ref. 8, 9
01-09-1913, 29:26
117W46, 33N50

Nixon's exact birth time has been determined by -N- values using the following events:

-*-,	06-21-1940	Marriage to Pat
-*-,	11-05-1946	Election to US House
-*-,	11-07-1950	Election to US Senate
-*-,	09-23-1952	Checkers Speech
-*-,	11-04-1952	Election to US vice-presidency
-*-,	11-05-1968	Election to US presidency
-*-,	02-21-1972	Visit to China
-*-,	05-22-1972	Watergate Break-in
-*-,	08-09-1974	Resignation from presidency

With these events the resulting -N- values show a large peak at a UT = 29:26.

Franklin D. Roosevelt   Ref. 10
01-30-1882, 25:45

George Washington (Given in the introduction to this appendix.)

Canada   Ref. 11
07-01-1867, 05:00
75W42, 45N25

Mexico   Ref. 12
09-16-1810, 18:00 (noon)

United States of America   Ref. 13
07-04-1776, 22:00

There are many times used for the birth of the US by various astrologers. I have based my time on the discussion given in Ref. 13 which supports a UT = 22:00. If the -N- values are calculated for the following events, a peak is observed at a UT = 22:00. A higher peak is observed twelve hours earlier, but that time is inconsistent with the historical information.

-*-,	05-10-1869	Transcontinental railroad
-*-,	08-15-1914	Panama Canal
-*-,	07-16-1945	Trinity atom bomb
-*-,	07-20-1969	Landing on the Moon
-S-,	06-18-1812	War of 1812
-S-,	04-12-1861	Civil War
-S-,	04-20-1898	Spanish-American War
-S-,	04-06-1917	World War I
-S-,	12-07-1941	Pearl Harbor
-S-,	06-27-1950	Korean War

Chapter III — Natal Information
Adolf Hitler   Ref. 14
04-20-1889, 17:34
13E02, 48N15

Hitler's -N- values have been calculated for the following events:

-I-,	05-25-1913,	12	Arrival in Munich
-S-,	10-05-1916,	20	Wounding in leg
-*-,	11-08-1923,	20	Beer Hall Putsch
-I-,	01-30-1933,	11.5	Becomes chancellor
-*-,	09-01-1939,	4.75	Invasion of Poland
-S-,	06-22-1941,	4	Invasion of Russia
-*-,	04-30-1945,	15	Death

The -N- values are shown in Figure A-5 for two sets of W, Tran for a span of time somewhat longer than is required by the historically recorded information. The highest peak is used for the results in this book.

German Empire   Ref. 15
01-18-1871, 13:00

Hitler Birth Scan

−N→
Intensities Normalized to One

W=0.5, Tran=6,14
W=1.0, Tran=10,14

Universal Time in Decimal Hours

Figure A−5

German Reichstag   Ref. 16
   4-14-1871, 12:00 (noon)

Chapter IV — Natal Information

Joseph Stalin   Ref. 17
01-02-1880, 06:00

People's Republic of China   Ref. 18
10-01-1949, 07:12
116E28, 39N54

The following events have been used to calculate -N- values for the PRC:

- S -,	10-25-1950	PRC enters Korean War
- * -,	05-02-1956	Mao's "100 Flowers Bloom" Speech
- S -,	02-27-1957	Mao's "Contradictions" Speech
- S -,	06-19-1957	Publication of the "Contradictions" Speech
- S -,	10-25-1962	India — PRC war
- S -,	11-10-1965	Campaign against Wu Han begins — Cultural Revolution
- * -,	08-18-1966	Peking assembly of Red Guards
- * -,	09-25-1971	Admitted to the UN
- * -,	02-21-1972	Visit by US President Nixon
- * -,	09-09-1976	Death of Mao

The -N- values show a peak at UT = 7:12 which is consistent with the historical information that the ceremony conducted by Mao in Peking at Red Square took place shortly after 3:00 PM local time. Note that the Moon is conjunct the Ascendant to within a degree. If -N- values are calculated for the above events but the angles are not included, there is a high peak at UT = 8:30.

India   Ref. 19
08-14-1947, 18:30
77E12, 28N40

Union of Soviet Socialist Republics   Ref. 20
11-07-1917, 23:30

The Birth of the USSR took place in the evening. To determine the time of the birth, -N- values were calculated for the following events and a pronounced peak occurs at the time indicated:

- S -	08-09-1921	New Economic Policy
- S -	01-21-1924	Death of Lenin
- S -	12-05-1936	New Constitution

(continued next page)

- S -,	09-17-1939	USSR invasion of Poland
- S -,	06-22-1941	Invasion by Germany
- S -,	10-01-1949	Birth of PRC
- * -,	10-04-1957	*Sputnik I*
- * -,	04-12-1961	Human in orbit
- S -,	10-15-1964	Resignation of Khrushchev

Chapter V — Natal Information

Hashemite Dynasty   Ref. 21
04-01-1921, 10:00 (noon)

Egypt   Ref. 22
06-18-1953, 20:00
30E15, 30N03

The public announcement of the birth of the new Egyptian government was made five minutes after the time given above. The time we want is when the final decisions and document signing occurred. This would have been during the meeting and just before the public announcement. The following events have been used to determine -N- values for Egypt:

-S-,	06-23-1956,	10	Vote for new Constitution
-S-,	10-29-1956,	4	War
-S-,	06-05-1967,	4	War
-S-,	11-24-1968,	10	Closing of universities
-S-,	09-28-1970,	10	Death of Nasser
-S-,	07-18-1972,	10	Withdrawal of USSR advisers
-S-,	10-06-1973,	12	War
-S-,	11-19-1977,	10	Sadat's visit to Israel
-S-,	03-26-1979,	17	Camp David accords
-S-,	10-06-1981,	11	Death of Sadat

The Egyptian -N- values are shown in Figure A-6 for three sets of W, Tran. There are two peaks shortly before the public announcement at 10:05 PM local time. The first peak at UT = 19.8 corresponds to placing the MC trine the natal Sun. Considering that the Egyptian Constitution was voted into power, Nasser died and Sadat died with Saturn, Neptune and Uranus respectively at this MC position, UT = 19.8 is a reasonable choice. However I have chosen the peak at UT = 20.0 since the connection to the Sun is strong enough without involving the MC; the MC is close in any case, the peak at UT = 20.0 is explained; and the value is consistent with historical information as recorded. Note that the peak at UT = 20.3 is related to a Pluto emphasis.

Iran-Pahlavian Dynasty   Ref. 23
12-12-1925, 09:00 (noon)

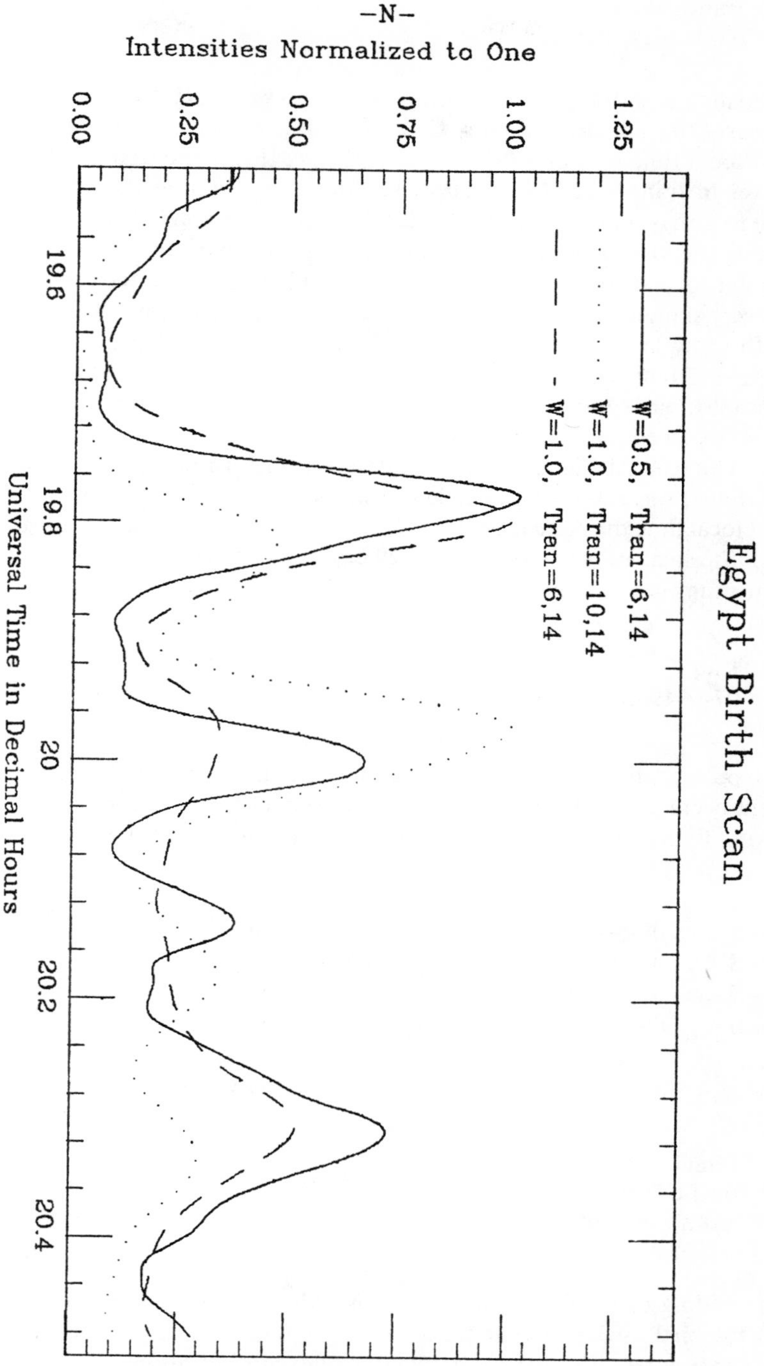

Egypt Birth Scan

-N-
Intensities Normalized to One

W=0.5, Tran=6,14
W=1.0, Tran=10,14
W=1.0, Tran=6,14

Universal Time in Decimal Hours
Figure A-6

Iran-Khomeini   Ref. 24
02-01-1979, 05:38

In dealing with Iran, the question is: When do we switch from the Pahlavian
Dynasty to the Khomeini era? Clearly Khomeini's arrival in Tehran at 9:08
AM local time on 02-01-1979 is too early, yet this is the time for his taking
power in Iran. What I have chosen to do is to switch at the start of 1982.
The reason is that the Iran-Pahlavian Dynasty -S- graph indicates, with three
peaks, the loss of power to Khomeini, the problems with the militants, and
the start of war between Iran and Iraq. Beginning with 1982, the two -S- graphs
are very similar through 1989 except that the Iran-Khomeini values are higher.
Both show large changes in late 1987 and early 1988. Their -I- graphs are
quite different with the Iran-Khomeini values and peaks being higher. Conceptually, what I am saying is that it took several years for the old patterns
to be replaced by the new ones.
       The 9:08 AM local time is the time Khomeini's plane touched down in
Tehran. It was several minutes later that he stepped from the plane. At 9:21
AM local time the Ascendant was zero degrees Aries. The Iran-Iraq war began
with the solar progressed Moon in 29 degrees of Aries for this chart and the
transiting Sun conjunct Saturn at zero degrees of Libra.

Iraq   Ref. 25
07-14-1958, 04:30

The public announcement of the coup in Iraq that set up its present government occurred at 7:00 PM. However, the coup occurred in the early morning
hours. I have used -N- values to set a time. The events used are given below:

- S -,   02-8-1963   *Coup* by Abdel-Salam Arif
- S -,   02-10-1973   Crisis with Pakistan
- S -,   07-01-1973   Serious *coup* attempt
- S -,   09-22-1980   Iran-Iraq war

The is a single large peak at UT = 4:30 for the day of the coup.

Israel   Ref. 26
05-14-1948, 14:32
34E45, 32N07

The ending of the British mandate for Palestine did not set the exact time
for the birth of Israel. The time was set by the events discussed in Ref. 26.
To confirm Israel's birth time, two sets of events have been used, along with

two sets of W, and Tran. The sets are given below:

Event Set A
  - S -, 10-29-1956,   5 War
  - S -, 06-05-1967   5 War
  - S -, 10-06-1973   12 War

Event Set B
  - I -, 05-11-1949, 17 Join UN
  - S -, 10-29-1956,   5 War
  - S -, 06-05-1967,   5 War
  - S -, 10-06-1973, 12 War
  - S -, 11-19-1977, 10 Sadat's visit
  - S -, 03-26-1979, 17 Camp David accords

The resultant -N- values are shown in Figures A-7 and A-8. Clearly using more events helps in clarifying the natal birthtime. The peak in the -N- values is to within a minute of the historical time of 4:32 PM.

        Jordan   Ref. 27
        03-22-1946, 12:00 (noon)

The crowning of King Hussein was not the birth of modern Jordan. Jordan took part in the world as an independent nation, on the date given above, at the treaty releasing Jordan from Great Britain's hold.

        Lebanon   Ref. 28
        11-22-1943, 10:00 (noon)

During the course of this day, with their release from jail, the Lebanese leaders took political control of the country from the French. See also Syria below.

        Libya   Ref. 29
        09-01-1969, 10:00 (noon)

        Saudi Arabia   Ref. 30
        10-06-1932, 10:00 (noon)

        Syria   Ref. 31
        06-21-1945, 10:00 (noon)

Following Lebanon's action in late 1943, Syria also took political control from the French. However, the French remained in both countries with military and technical forces. Effective on the date given for Syria, both

Israel Birth Scan --- Event Set A

Intensities Normalized to One

−N−

W=0.5, Tran=6,14

W=1.0, Tran=10,14

Universal Time in Decimal Hours

Figure A−7

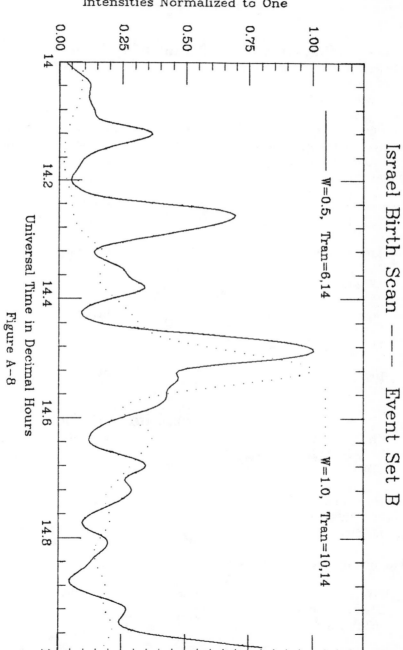

Israel Birth Scan ——— Event Set B

Intensities Normalized to One

—N—

W=0.5, Tran=6,14

W=1.0, Tran=10,14

Universal Time in Decimal Hours

Figure A-8

countries began removing all French forces. They also began participating in the world political and economic arena without French domination of their actions. The birth date given for Syria can appropriately be used as a second date of birth for Lebanon.

Chapter VI — Natal Information

Bretton Woods Conference   Ref. 32
07-22-1944, 26:43
71W26, 44N15

At the time the final vote was taken on setting up a new world banking system, the Ascendant was zero degrees Aries. Two minutes after the vote, the results of the conference were announced to the US with a live radio broadcast from Bretton Woods.

European Economic Community   Ref. 33
01-01-1958, 12:00 (noon)

International Monetary Fund and   Ref. 34
World Bank: Start
12-27-1945, 19:00

Organization of Petroleum   Ref. 35
    Exporting Countries
09-14-1960, 10:00 (noon)

Treaty   Ref. 36
03-25-1957, 18:00

Chapter VII — Natal Information

Chicago Reactor   Ref. 37
12-02-1942, 20:25
87W37, 41N49

Hiroshima   Ref. 38
08-05-1945, 23:15:30
132E25, 34N22

Note that the local date is 08-06-1945.

Hydrogen Bomb   Ref. 39
10-31-1952, 19:15
162E15, 11N30

Note that the local date is 11-01-1952.

Sputnik I   Ref. 40
10-04-1957, 21:00

Trinity   Ref. 41
07-16-1945, 11:29
106W00, 32N55

Note that Ref. 39 has the UT wrong for Trinity because war time was not taken properly into account.

USSR Atom Bomb   Ref. 42
08-29-1949, 04:00

Early morning was chosen for the UT for this nativity because most initial tests of nuclear weapons were done in the early morning near sunrise.

Chapter VIII — Natal Information

League of Nations (given in the introduction to this appendix)

San Francisco Conference   Ref. 43
    for the United Nations
06-25-1945, 29:53
122W25, 37N47

United Nations: Start   Ref. 44
10-24-1945, 21:50
77W00, 38N50

Chapter IX — Natal Information

West Germany   Ref. 45
09-07-1949, 10:00

DYNAMIC ASTROLOGY ALGORITHMS

The algorithms used to calculate all of the -I- and -S- graphs used in this book are given in this appendix. As with Appendix A, I will assume that the reader is familiar with basic astrology and algebra. After the detailed presentation of the algorithms, I will give a discussion of some of their salient features.

The -I- and -S- functions may be expressed as follows:

$$\text{-I-} = \text{-I-(TN,TE)} = \text{IP} \times \text{IT} = \text{IP(TN,TP)} \times \text{IT(TN,TE)}$$

and

$$\text{-S-} = \text{-S-(TN,TE)} = \text{SP} \times \text{ST} = \text{SP(TN,TP)} \times \text{ST(TN,TE)}$$

where:

TN   is the natal time in days.

TP   is the solar progressed time which is approximately TN + the entity's age in years.
(see Chapter I for the reference for TP)

TE   is the event time in days. For the graphs in the chapters, fifty event times a year have been calculated.

IP and SP are calculated using the progressions. IT and ST are calculated using the transits. The taking of the product of IP and IT to form -I-, and SP and ST to form -S-, is discussed in detail later in this appendix and in Chapter I.

The functions IP, IT, SP and ST are all sums of many terms. There is a term in the sum for each aspect used and for every possible pair of planets and angles used. The terms are all made up of three factors:

1) The first factor depends on the aspect.
2) The second factor depends on the two planets involved in forming the aspect.
3) The third factor depends on how close the aspect is to being exact.

The first two factors are held in arrays. The third factor is determined by a function which depends on the aspect angle and the planetary positions.

To make the notation clear, the three planetary arrays will be given first and then the three factors will be given. For the three times of interest, **TN**, **TP** and **TE**, arrays of planetary positions are calculated. For TN, the angles are also calculated if the exact time of birth is known. Algorithms for the calculation of planetary positions and the angles will not be given in this book because they are readily available from other sources. (For two sources, see the Matrix Software and Astro-Graphics Services order forms in the back of this book.) The three arrays of planetary positions and angles are:

Time	Array
TN	HNATL(j)
TP	HPROG(j or k)
TE	HTRAN(k)

Values of the dummy variables j or k

j or k	Planet or Angle	Abbreviation
1	Vertex	VT
2	Ascendant	AS
3	Midheaven	MC
4	North Node	NO
5	Moon	MO
6	Sun	SU
7	Mercury	ME
8	Venus	VE
9	Mars	MA
10	Jupiter	JU
11	Saturn	SA
12	Uranus	UR
13	Neptune	NE
14	Pluto	PL

Note that the node used in these calculations is the mean node of the Moon.

The three factors will now be given.

Aspects Used and the First Factors

The angles used for aspects in the -I- calculation are in the array **ANI(i)**. The angle related weighting factors are in the array **ZI(i)**. The values of ZI (and ZS for the -S- aspects) are set by the aspect involved for each term. The aspects are labeled by i. The aspects are in general weighted differently for each angle.

-I- Aspects and First Factors

i	ANI(i)	ZI(i)
1	0.	1.
2	120.	$1.5 \div 3\frac{2}{3}$
3	-120.	$1.5 \div 3\frac{2}{3}$
4	72.	$1.5 \div 5$
5	-72.	$1.5 \div 5$
6	144.	$1.5 \div 5$
7	-144.	$1.5 \div 5$
8	51.4286	$1.5 \div 7$
9	-51.4286	$1.5 \div 7$
10	102.8571	$1.5 \div 7$
11	-102.8571	$1.5 \div 7$
12	154.2857	$1.5 \div 7$
13	-154.2857	$1.5 \div 7$
14	40.	$1.5 \div 9$
15	-40.	$1.5 \div 9$
16	80.	$1.5 \div 9$
17	-80.	$1.5 \div 9$
18	160.	$1.5 \div 9$
19	-160.	$1.5 \div 9$

The angles used for aspects in the -S- calculation are in the array **ANS(i)**. The angle related weighting factors are in the array **ZS(i)**:

-S- Aspects and First Factors

i	ANS(i)	ZS(i)
1	0	1
2	180	1
3	90	$1 \div 1.5$
4	-90	$1 \div 1.5$
5	45	$1 \div 4$
6	-45	$1 \div 4$

7	135	$1 \div 4$
8	-135	$1 \div 4$
9	30	$1 \div 4$
10	-30	$1 \div 4$
11	60	$1 \div 4$
12	-60	$1 \div 4$
13	120	$1 \div 4$
14	-120	$1 \div 4$
15	150	$1 \div 4$
16	-150	$1 \div 4$

Second Factors

These are arrays of weights that are determined by the two planets involved in the aspect. The aspect, i, is considered only to the point of keeping conjunctions, $i = 1$, separate from all other aspects, (i .NE. 1). The weights are sometimes different for progressions and transits. The indices j and k refer to planets or angles.

-I- Second Factors

$IARP(i = 1, j, k)$

j Value and Planet	k Value and Planet										
	4 NO	5 MO	6 SU	7 ME	8 VE	9 MA	10 JU	11 SA	12 UR	13 NE	14 PL
1 VT	1	2	3	3	3	3	3	1	2	2	2
2 AS	1	6	9	9	9	9	9	2	7	5	6
3 MC	1	6	9	9	9	9	9	2	7	5	6
4 NO	0	1	1	1	1	1	1	1	1	1	1
5 MO	1	9	9	2	8	7	9	1	9	3	8
6 SU	1	4	7	1	2	1	8	1	9	2	7
7 ME	1	1	2	8	7	8	9	2	9	3	7
8 VE	1	2	8	7	9	1	9	2	9	3	7
9 MA	1	1	7	8	1	9	9	2	3	4	8
10 JU	1	8	9	9	9	9	9	2	9	5	7
11 SA	1	1	1	2	2	2	2	3	1	2	2
12 UR	1	9	9	9	9	3	9	1	9	7	7
13 NE	1	2	3	3	3	4	5	2	7	9	9
14 PL	1	7	8	7	8	7	2	7	7	9	1

IARP(i .NE. 1, j, k) and
IART(i .NE. 1, j, k)

j Value and Planet	k Value and Planet										
	4 NO	5 MO	6 SU	7 ME	8 VE	9 MA	10 JU	11 SA	12 UR	13 NE	14 PL
1 VT	0	3	3	3	3	3	3	1	3	3	3
2 AS	1	9	9	9	9	9	9	3	9	9	9
3 MC	1	9	9	9	9	9	9	3	9	9	9
4 NO	1	1	1	1	1	1	1	0	1	1	1
5 MO	1	9	9	9	9	9	9	3	9	9	9
6 SU	1	9	9	9	9	9	9	3	9	9	9
7 ME	1	9	9	9	9	9	9	3	9	9	9
8 VE	1	9	9	9	9	9	9	3	9	9	9
9 MA	1	9	9	9	9	9	9	3	9	9	9
10 JU	1	9	9	9	9	9	9	3	9	9	9
11 SA	1	3	3	3	3	3	3	3	3	3	3
12 UR	1	9	9	9	9	9	9	3	9	9	9
13 NE	1	9	9	9	9	9	9	3	9	9	9
14 PL	1	9	9	9	9	9	9	3	9	9	9

IART(i = 1, j, k)

j Value and Planet	k Value and Planet										
	4 NO	5 MO	6 SU	7 ME	8 VE	9 MA	10 JU	11 SA	12 UR	13 NE	14 PL
1 VT	1	8	3	3	3	3	3	1	2	2	2
2 AS	1	8	9	9	9	9	9	2	7	5	6
3 MC	1	8	9	9	9	9	9	2	7	5	6
4 NO	1	8	1	1	1	1	1	1	1	1	1
5 MO	1	8	9	2	8	7	9	1	9	3	8
6 SU	1	8	7	1	2	1	8	1	9	2	7
7 ME	1	8	2	8	7	8	9	2	9	3	7
8 VE	1	8	8	7	9	1	9	2	9	3	7
9 MA	1	8	7	8	1	9	9	2	3	4	8
10 JU	1	8	9	9	9	9	9	2	9	5	7
11 SA	1	8	1	2	2	2	2	3	1	2	2
12 UR	1	8	9	9	9	3	9	1	9	7	7
13 NE	1	8	3	3	3	4	5	2	7	9	9
14 PL	1	8	8	7	8	7	2	7	7	9	1

-S- Second Factors

SARP(i = 1, j, k)

j Value and Planet	k Value and Planet										
	4 NO	5 MO	6 SU	7 ME	8 VE	9 MA	10 JU	11 SA	12 UR	13 NE	14 PL
1 VT	1	1	3	4	4	4	5	8	6	6	4
2 AS	1	4	7	8	8	8	6	9	9	6	4
3 MC	1	1	3	5	4	8	7	9	9	6	4
4 NO	0	3	3	2	2	2	2	2	2	2	2
5 MO	1	0	3	4	2	7	2	8	8	8	6
6 SU	1	3	0	1	1	3	3	7	6	7	4
7 ME	1	2	1	0	1	2	4	7	7	5	4
8 VE	1	2	1	2	0	8	3	8	7	6	5
9 MA	1	6	3	4	8	0	2	9	8	7	6
10 JU	1	3	2	3	3	2	0	7	5	5	5
11 SA	1	9	7	8	7	9	7	0	9	7	8
12 UR	1	9	7	7	8	7	5	9	0	4	8
13 NE	1	4	7	8	8	9	8	7	4	0	6
14 PL	1	7	4	4	6	7	4	8	4	4	0

SARP(i .NE. 1, j,k)

j Value and Planet	k Value and Planet										
	4 NO	5 MO	6 SU	7 ME	8 VE	9 MA	10 JU	11 SA	12 UR	13 NE	14 PL
1 VT	1	1	3	4	4	4	5	8	6	6	4
2 AS	1	4	7	8	8	8	6	9	9	6	4
3 MC	1	1	3	5	4	8	7	9	9	6	4
4 NO	0	5	2	2	2	2	2	2	2	2	2
5 MO	1	2	7	3	4	8	4	9	9	9	9
6 SU	1	7	5	4	4	8	8	7	7	7	7
7 ME	1	6	4	8	6	9	9	9	9	9	9
8 VE	1	6	4	6	8	9	9	9	9	9	9
9 MA	1	5	8	9	9	9	9	9	9	9	9
10 JU	1	4	8	9	9	9	9	9	9	9	9
11 SA	1	9	9	9	9	9	9	9	9	9	9
12 UR	1	9	7	9	9	9	9	9	9	9	9
13 NE	1	9	7	9	9	9	9	9	9	9	9
14 PL	1	9	7	9	9	9	9	9	9	9	9

SART(i = 1, j, k)

j Value and Planet	k Value and Planet										
	4 NO	5 MO	6 SU	7 ME	8 VE	9 MA	10 JU	11 SA	12 UR	13 NE	14 PL
1 VT	1	7	1	2	2	2	2	4	4	4	4
2 AS	2	7	6	5	5	5	5	8	8	8	8
3 MC	2	7	6	5	5	5	5	8	8	8	8
4 NO	1	7	1	2	2	2	2	2	2	2	2
5 MO	1	7	2	3	3	3	4	9	6	7	7
6 SU	1	7	2	5	5	7	5	9	8	8	7
7 ME	1	7	3	5	5	5	5	9	7	7	6
8 VE	1	7	2	5	5	8	5	9	7	6	8
9 MA	1	7	5	5	8	5	5	9	8	7	8
10 JU	1	7	4	5	5	5	5	7	5	5	5
11 SA	1	7	8	8	7	9	7	9	9	8	8
12 UR	1	7	6	7	8	7	5	9	8	6	8
13 NE	1	7	6	8	8	9	8	7	4	8	6
14 PL	1	7	6	6	6	7	4	8	4	4	8

SART(i .NE. 1, j, k)

j Value and Planet	k Value and Planet										
	4 NO	5 MO	6 SU	7 ME	8 VE	9 MA	10 JU	11 SA	12 UR	13 NE	14 PL
1 VT	1	3	1	2	2	2	2	4	4	4	4
2 AS	2	7	4	5	5	5	5	8	8	8	8
3 MC	2	7	4	5	5	5	5	8	8	8	8
4 NO	1	3	4	2	2	2	2	2	2	2	2
5 MO	1	7	4	5	5	7	5	9	8	8	7
6 SU	1	7	4	5	5	5	5	9	6	7	7
7 ME	1	7	4	5	5	5	5	9	7	7	6
8 VE	1	7	4	5	5	8	5	9	7	6	8
9 MA	1	7	4	5	8	5	5	9	8	7	8
10 JU	1	7	4	5	5	5	5	7	5	5	5
11 SA	1	7	4	7	8	7	9	7	9	9	8
12 UR	1	7	4	7	8	7	5	9	8	6	8
13 NE	1	7	4	8	8	9	8	7	4	8	6
14 PL	1	7	4	4	6	7	4	8	4	4	8

Third Factors

The third factors are determined by how many degrees the two planets making the aspect under consideration are from making the aspect exactly. There is a parameter, W, involved which sets the orb. A more detailed discussion of W is given later. There are several functions used in the calculation of the third factors:

$y = MOD(x)$ For any angle x, the function MOD operating on x returns the angle in the range from 0 to 360 degrees. For example, if x is -20 degrees, then MOD(-20) is equal to 340 degrees.

$y = ABS(x)$ y is the absolute value of x, i.e. $y = |x|$.

$y = DIF(a,b,c)$ $y = ABS(c-MOD(a-b))$; however if y is greater than 180, then $y = 360-y$.

$y = ORB(x)$ $y = e^{-(ABS(x)/W)^3}$ The value of W is in general variable. See Appendix A and the discussion below.

    The full expressions for the third factors will be given in terms of the ORB and DIF functions plus the planetary and aspect arrays. The expressions for the third factors are given with the expressions for IP, IT, SP and ST in the next section.

IP, IT, SP and ST

    The expressions for IP, IT, SP and ST can now be given. I will discuss the limits on the sums after the expressions are given.

-I- = IP × IT

$$IP = \sum_{i=1}^{19} \sum_{j=5}^{14} \sum_{k=4}^{14} ZI(i) \times IARP(i, j, k) \times ORB(IDNP(i, j, k))$$

$$+ \tfrac{1}{2} \times (\sum_{i=1}^{19} \sum_{j=nn}^{4} \sum_{k=4}^{14} ZI(i) \times IARP(i, j, k) \times ORB(IDNP(i, j, k))$$

$$+ \sum_{i=1}^{19} \sum_{j=nn}^{4} \sum_{k=4}^{14} ZI(i) \times IARP(i, j, k) \times ORB(IDNP180(i, j, k)))$$

(continued next page)

$$+ 2 \times (\sum_{i=1}^{19} \sum_{j=5}^{14} \sum_{k=j+1}^{14} ZI(i) \times IARP(i, j, k) \times ORB(IDPP(i, j, k))$$

$$+ \tfrac{1}{2} \times (\sum_{i=1}^{19} \sum_{j=4}^{4} \sum_{k=j+1}^{14} ZI(i) \times IARP(i, j, k) \times ORB(IDPP(i, j, k))$$

$$+ \sum_{i=1}^{19} \sum_{j=4}^{4} \sum_{k=j+1}^{14} ZI(i) \times IARP(i, j, k) \times ORB(IDPP180(i, j, k))))$$

where:

$$IDNP(i, j, k) = DIF(ANI(i),HNATL(j),HPROG(k))$$
$$IDPP(i, j, k) = DIF(ANI(i),HPROG(j),HPROG(k))$$
$$IDNP180(i, j, k) = DIF(ANI(i),(MOD(HNATL(j) + 180)),HPROG(k))$$
$$IDPP180(i, j, k) = DIF(ANI(i),(MOD(HPROG(j) + 180)),HPROG(k))$$

$$IT = \sum_{i=1}^{19} \sum_{j=5}^{14} \sum_{k=nt \text{ and } k=4}^{14} ZI(i) \times IART(i, j, k) \times ORB(IDNT(i, j, k))$$

$$+ \tfrac{1}{2} \times (\sum_{i=1}^{19} \sum_{j=nn}^{4} \sum_{k=nt \text{ and } k=4}^{14} ZI(i) \times IART(i, j, k) \times ORB(IDNT(i, j, k))$$

$$+ \sum_{i=1}^{19} \sum_{j=nn}^{4} \sum_{k=nt \text{ and } k=4}^{14} ZI(i) \times IART(i, j, k) \times ORB(IDNT180(i, j, k)))$$

where:

$$IDNT(i, j, k) = DIF(ANI(i),HNATL(j),HTRAN(k))$$

$$IDNT180(i, j, k) = DIF(ANI(i),(MOD(HNATL(j) + 180)),HTRAN(k))$$

-S- = SP × ST

$$SP = \sum_{i=1}^{16} \sum_{j=nn}^{14} \sum_{k=4}^{14} ZS(i) \times SARP(i, j, k) \times ORB(SDNP(i, j, k))$$

$$+ 2 \times \sum_{i=1}^{16} \sum_{j=4}^{14} \sum_{k=j+1}^{14} ZS(i) \times SARP(i, j, k) \times ORB(SDPP(i, j, k))$$

where:

$SDNP(i, j, k) = DIF(ANS(i),HNATL(j),HPROG(k))$

$SDPP(i, j, k) = DIF(ANS(i),HPROG(j),HPROG(k))$

and,

$$ST = \sum_{i=1}^{16} \sum_{j=nn}^{14} \sum_{\substack{k=nt\ and\ k=4}}^{14} ZS(i) \times SART(i, j, k) \times ORB(SDNT(i, j, k))$$

where:

$SDNT(i, j, k) = DIF(ANS(i),HNATL(j),HTRAN(k))$

DETAILED DISCUSSION

Structure of the Sums

The -I- sums have more terms then the -S- sums. The reason is that the Descendant, Anti-vertex and South Node of the Moon must be taken into account. In the -S- sums this is done by the opposition aspect. In the -I- sums there is no opposition aspect present. The solution is that 180 degrees is added to the angles and North Node of the Moon and the sums are calculated again. The factors of one half in IP and IT are to prevent the angles and nodes from being too dominant in the final values. The factors of two are discussed below.

To prevent a meaningless spike in the -I- and -S- values when TE is very close to TN, conjunctions of the transiting planets to themselves in the natal chart are not allowed until the transiting planets have made nearly one circuit of the zodiac.

Limits on the Sums

i   The i limits are simply set to cover the full array of angles used for the aspects.

j   If the j index refers to natal planets and angles, then the j limits go from nn to 14. If the natal angles are included, nn is equal to one; nn is equal to four if the natal angles are not included. If j refers to progressed planets, then the lower limit on the j sum is always four. The upper limit is four for the angles and Moon's Nodes sums in IP and IT, and 14 otherwise.

k   The k limits for progressions are four to 14. For transits, the k limits range from nt to 14 except k = 5 (the Moon) is not included but k = 4

(the Moon's Nodes) is included. nt is always six or greater otherwise. In all of the graphs of -I- and -S- given in the chapters, nt is
equal to ten. A few of the -N- scans shown in Appendix A have nt
equal to six.

In general, all of the limits can be varied so as to leave out or include
either the fast- or slow-moving angles and/or planets. For consistency of
presentation, the limits have been fixed at the indicated values for all of the
graphs in the chapters of this book. This means that all of the planets and
nodes of the Moon are used for the natal and progressed times, TN and TP.
The natal angles are used as noted. For the transiting planets at time TE,
only Jupiter through Pluto and the nodes of the Moon are used except for
some -N- values in Appendix A. When the inner planets are included, the
-I- and -S- values vary day to day. Using Jupiter on out for the transiting
planets means that the -I- and -S- values vary week to week. This rate of variation is more convenient for observing the twenty-year time spans used in the
chapters.

In the IP and SP sums, a factor of two multiplies the sums of the terms
of the progressed planets making aspects to the progressed planets. This factor accounts for the fact that the k index of these sums begins at $j + 1$. If
the k sum had been begun at $k = 6$, then the factor of two would not be required, but the computational time would be slightly longer. With this factor
of two, the possible contribution of the aspects of the progressed planets making aspects to progressed planets, is the same as that of the natal planets making aspects to progressed planets.

Aspects and the First Factor

The aspects in the array ANI(i) come from multiples of 360 degrees divided
by the odd numbers 1, 3, 5, 7 and 9. Note that 360 degrees is also zero degrees.
In conventional terms, the resulting aspects are referred to as conjunctions
in the first, third, fifth, seventh and ninth harmonic charts. Additional research
may indicate that higher harmonics are important. However, if the higher
harmonics were used, the orb parameter, W, would need to vary with the harmonic. The weighting factors, ZI(i), associated with each harmonic are different. They are set in part to take into account the number of aspects
generated in each harmonic.

The aspects in the array ANS(i) come from 360 degrees divided by the
numbers 1, 2, 4, 6, 8 and 12. Because these numbers can all be generated
by the prime numbers 1, 2 and 3, there is significant repetition in the conjunctions in the related harmonic charts. The resulting aspects are the ones
most commonly used by astrologers. The weighting factors, ZS(i), were determined by experimentation, as is mentioned in Chapter I. Clearly, as with the
odd-number related harmonics, the aspects coming from higher numbers are
weighted less.

Planets and the Second Factor

A weighting factor is present in the arrays of the second factor for every possible combination of planets and/or angles used. The choice of the scale of these planet and angle specific weighting factors sets the scale of the final -I- and -S- values. The scale was chosen to vary from zero to nine for programming convenience and adequate dynamic range. The exact values given have been chosen from my personal observations. Note that only conjunctions have been treated separately from the other aspects.

Orbs and the Third Factor

The orb used is set by the choice of the ORB function. I considered several ORB functions of the form:

$$y = e^{-(|x|/W)^n} \qquad n = 1, 2, 3, 4, \ldots$$

For $W = 1.0$, the values of these functions are shown in Figure B-1 for $n = 1$, 2 and 3. I chose $n = 3$ so that the contributions from an aspect would fall off quickly to zero if the value of $|x|$ was much larger than W.

For all of the graphs in the chapters, W is taken to be equal to one. In Appendix A, a few values of $W = 0.5$ are shown for some -N- graphs. A general concept is that the more angles, planets and aspects that are used, the smaller W should be. If W is too large, then too many aspects are being made all of the time. A variation of W with the harmonic of the aspect was not found to be necessary or desirable to obtain significant results. Note that if W were made to vary with the harmonic of the aspect, the first factors would probably need to be changed. As to the choice for W, my personal astrological observations indicated that when aspects are accurate to within a degree, they are the strongest for all of the harmonics used. Possibly most important, I am pragmatic; $W = 1.0$ works very well for $nt = 10$ and the twenty-year time spans.

A Comment on the Original Choices for Weights

As is discussed in Chapter I, the angle weighting factors and the planet weighting factors were only adjusted during the time I used the three individuals' charts to develop the -I- and -S- graphs. These three individual's graphs are not in this book. I also used the graphs coming from the chart of one country in my development of the Dynamic Astrology graphs. I checked only two things with this country's graphs: that a factor of two should multiply the progressed planets making aspects with progressed planets as is discussed above; and, I also confirmed that taking the orb parameter $W = 1.0$ was the best choice for my purposes. The country I used was Israel. Otherwise, no parameters in the algorithms were adjusted once the calculations for this book were begun.

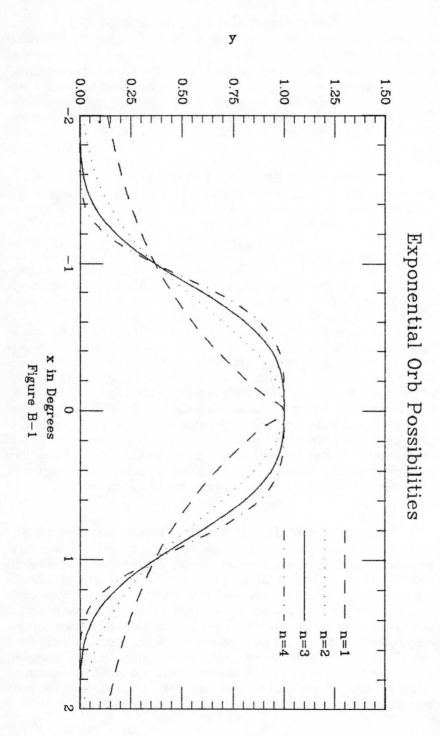

Exponential Orb Possibilities

x in Degrees
Figure B-1

IP, IT, SP and ST Combined

Conceptually, the terms in the expressions for IP, IT, SP and ST come from conventional astrology. In their analyses, astrologers use aspects and orbs for the planets and angles. Assigning numerical weights to each of the three factors and summing the terms is less conventional, but mathematically inclined astrologers have attempted similar things before. The innovative developments being presented in this book are first, that significant information on the changes in the lives of entities can be obtained if the IP, IT, SP and ST values are calculated with the particular expressions given. And second, that the intensity of the changes for an entity correlates with the entity's -I- and -S- values where -I- comes from taking the product of IP and IT, and -S- comes from taking the product of SP and ST.

The -I- and -S- values for group entities and entities with multiple births are calculated by taking further products of the -I- and -S- values as is discussed in Chapter I. To help you see why this is done, as well as see why products are taken between progressions and transits to form -I- and -S-, the following example is presented. Sums and products of IP, IT, SP and ST for the US and Franklin D. Roosevelt (FDR) are shown in the figures as indicated in the listing below:

Figure	Sum or Product
B- 2	IP(US) + IP(FDR)
B- 3	IT(US) + IT(FDR)
B- 4	IP(US) + IP(FDR) + IT(US) + IT(FDR)
B- 5	IP(US)*IP(FDR)
B- 6	IT(US)*IT(FDR)
II- 7	IP(US)*IP(FDR)*IT(US)*IT(FDR)/700/700
B- 7	SP(US) + SP(FDR)
B- 8	ST(US) + ST(FDR)
B- 9	SP(US) + SP(FDR) + ST(US) + ST(FDR)
B-10	SP(US)*SP(FDR)
B-11	ST(US)*ST(FDR)
II 8	SP(US)*SP(FDR)*ST(US)*ST(FDR)/700/700

The correlation of significant events in history with the combined -I- (Figure II-7) and -S- (Figure II-8) graphs of the US and FDR is discussed in Chapter II. The larger peaks in these two graphs would be expected to appear as peaks in some of the graphs of the terms going into the combined graphs, and they do appear. Studying Figures B-2 through B-11, observe that Roosevelt's winning the 1932 election for President appears as peaks in the IP sums and products, and the bombing of Pearl Harbor similarly appears in the ST sums and products. However, particularly in the graphs presenting sums, there are numerous other peaks which are sometimes higher. Some significant changes are without peaks and some peaks occur where major changes did not take place historically. In addition, the sums all have very high background levels. The figures that show clear and unambiguous peaks which correlate with major historical changes are Figures II-7 and II-8 (the combined US-Roosevelt -I- and -S- graphs).

The conclusion I draw from the above observations is that the IP, IT, SP and ST expressions and their various sums and products are themselves worthy of investigation. For example, some of them may be more indicative of activity level rather than changes. But, to see with clarity the intensity of changes, the -I- and -S- values are the places to begin one's analysis. Then the progressions and transits can be investigated separately, with the expressions above or the chart itself.

Angles

An orb of one degree, $W = 1.0$, has been used in the calculations for the graphs presented in the chapters of this book. This means that if the angles are being included in the algorithms, then the natal or birth time must be known to two, or at the most three, minutes of accuracy. This is because the angles move approximately one degree for every four minutes of birth time. If the natal time cannot be determined to the required accuracy by recorded historical information, -N- function analysis or other natal rectification procedures, then the angles should not be included in the use of the algorithms.

When I include the angles in a graph of -I- or -S- , I frequently also calculate the graph again without including the angles. In this way the contributions from the angles to the -I- or -S- values are easy to see. As an example of this procedure, I have recalculated the -S- graph for India without including the angles. The results are shown in Figure B-12. India's -S- graph with angles included is shown in Figure IV-9. The main difference between these two graphs is that leaving out the angles reduces the average value by approximately 15%. All of the major peaks are still present, but from peak to peak there are 20-40% variations in some cases. These results are typical as well as what is expected considering that the angles are in about 15% of the terms.

Natal Planet Sensitivities

The natal planet sensitivities are calculated by the simple procedure of doubling the contribution of every term in IP or SP with a j index value equal to the natal planet in question. This is done for each of the planets in turn and the new -I- or -S- values are compared with the standard value of -I- or -S- . The most sensitive natal planet is the one with the largest increase in -I- and/or -S- value.

Note that this procedure includes the sensitivity of the progressed planets as well as the natal planets for the event in question. The j index in IP and SP runs over both natal and progressed planets. The procedure does not look at the sensitivity to transiting planets individually, but changing the value of nt can change the result for the most sensitive natal (and progressed) planet.

Value

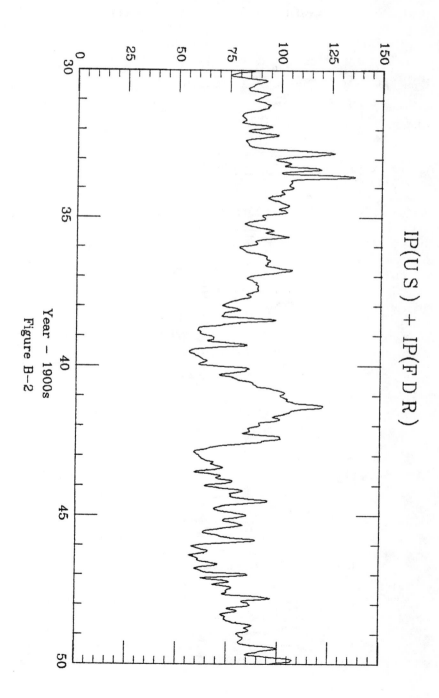

IP(U S) + IP(F D R)

Year – 1900s

Figure B-2

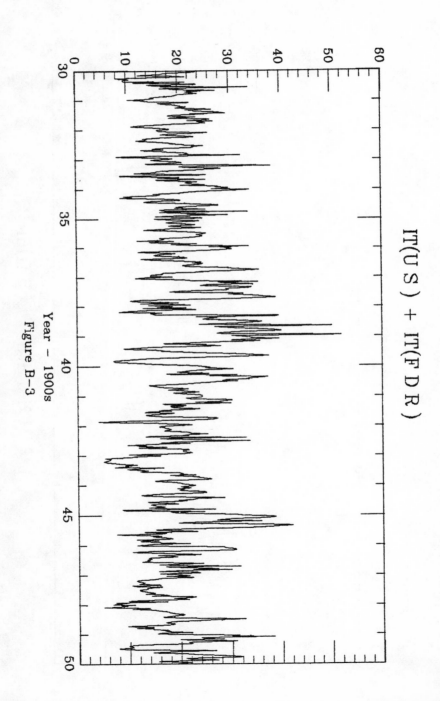

Value

IT(U S) + IT(F D R)

Year – 1900s

Figure B–3

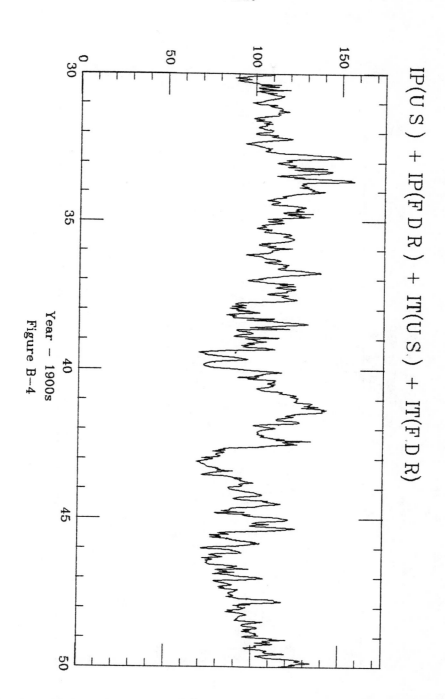

Value

IP(U S) + IP(F D R) + IT(U S) + IT(F D R)

Year – 1900s

Figure B–4

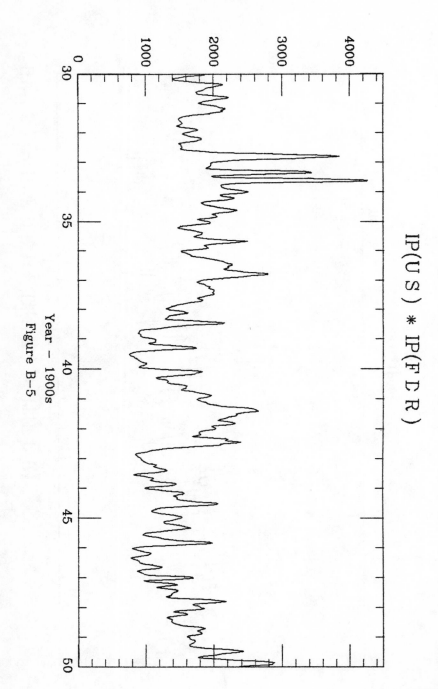

Value

IP(U S) * IP(F C R)

Year – 1900s

Figure B–5

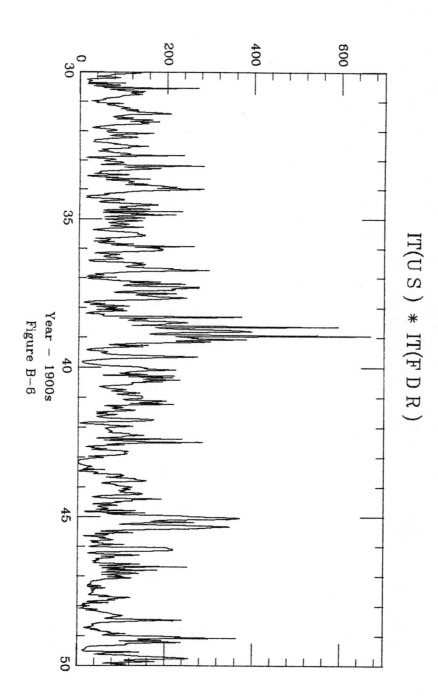

Value

IT(U S) * IT(F D R)

Year — 1900s

Figure B-6

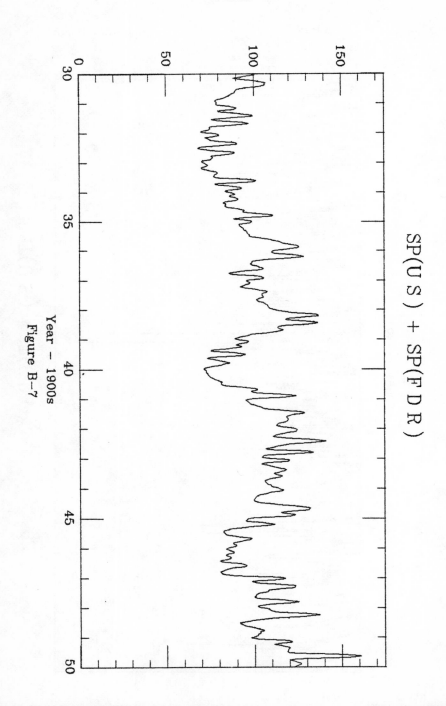

Value

SP(U S) + SP(F D R)

Year – 1900s

Figure B–7

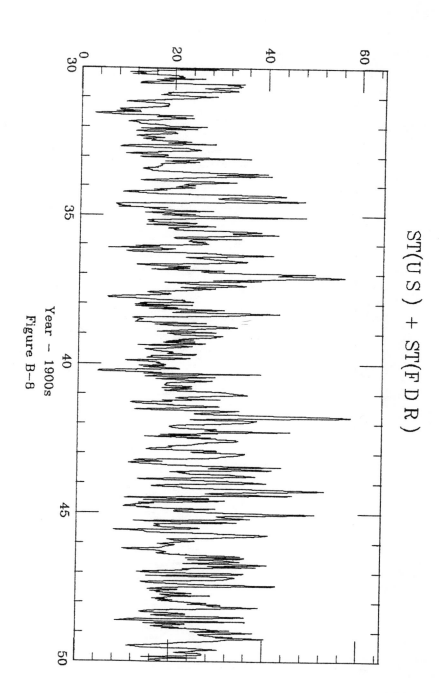

Value

ST(U S) + ST(F D R)

Year – 1900s

Figure B-8

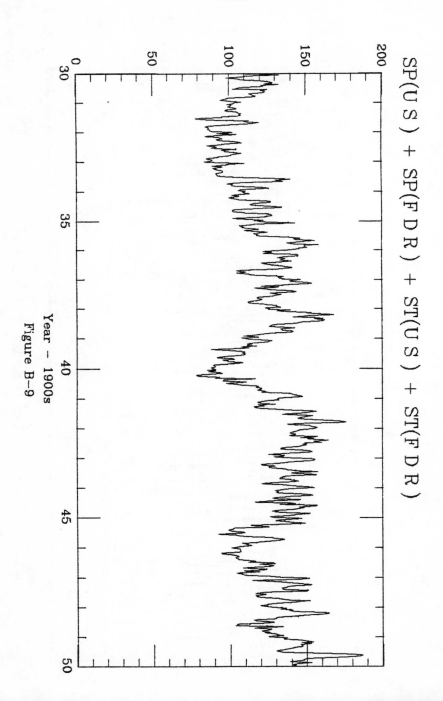

Year – 1900s

Figure B–9

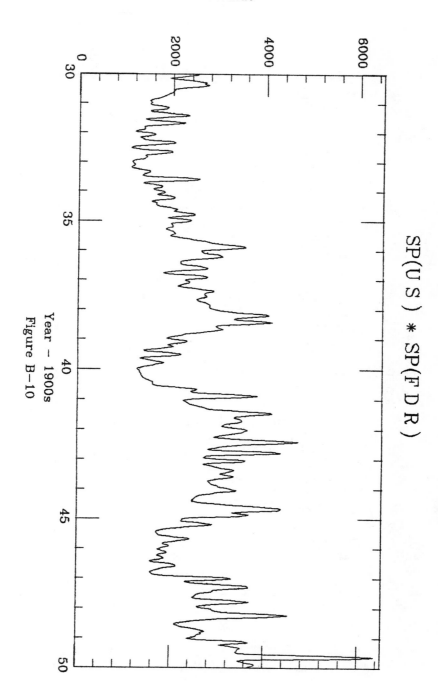

Value

SP(U S) * SP(F D R)

Year − 1900s

Figure B-10

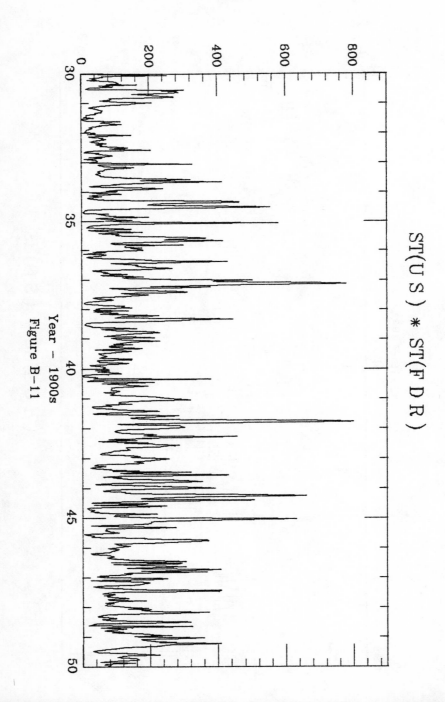

Value

ST(U S) * ST(F D R)

Year – 1900s
Figure B-11

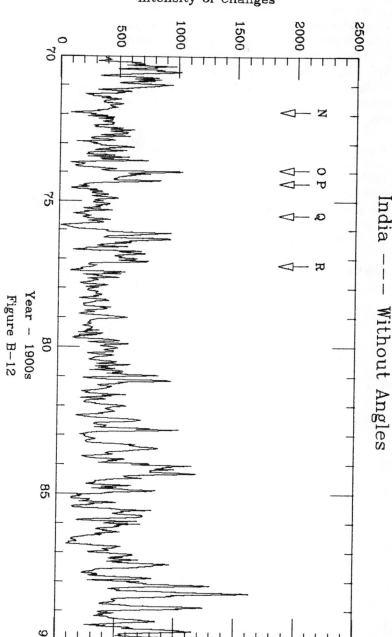

India --- Without Angles

-S-
Intensity of Changes

Year - 1900s
Figure B-12

Summary

All of the algorithms, inputs, referrals and references used to calculate all of the results presented in this book have been presented in the two appendices of the book. All of the historical information presented in the chapters is readily available from standard sources. I have observed that providing this level of detail and referrals to source material is an important step in the process of giving validity to the results presented.

My intent has been to produce a revolutionary astrology book of quality and clarity. The test of this book will be use of its results and methods by humanity. To this end, three methods for using Dynamic Astrology are provided:

1) the computer-oriented reader can program the algorithms from the information provided in this book
2) the graphs for any nativity may be ordered from Astro Computing Services
3) the algorithms are under development for most personal computers from Matrix Software or Astro-Graphics Services. The order forms are given on the following pages.

This book takes steps in new directions. We are part of a vast and creative universe. More steps can be taken and more new directions explored.

References

1. *New York Times*, 11 Jan 1920, p. 1.
2. Samuel Willard, *Old South Church*, Children Baptized (Boston: Old South Church Congregational Library, 14 Beacon St.), p. 54.
3. Paul L. Ford, *Many-sided Franklin*, (New York: Century, 1899), p. 1.
4. Leonard W. Labaree, et. al. Eds., *The Autobiography of Benjamin Franklin*, (New Haven: Yale, 1964), p. 47.
5. Dumas Malone, *Jefferson the Virginian*, (Boston: Little, Brown and Co., 1948), p. 3.
6. Richard M. Ketchum, *The World of George Washington*, (New York: American Heritage, 1974), p. 20.
7. William E. Barton, *The Women Lincoln Loved*, (Indianapolis: Bobbs-Merrill, 1927), p. 83.
8. Richard Blackmore Vaughan, *Astrology in Modern Language*, New York: G. P. Putnam's Sons, 1972), p. 341.
9. Doris Chase Doane, *Horoscopes of the U.S. Presidents*, (Professional Astrologers Incorporated, P.O. Box 2616, Hollywood, CA 90028, 1952, 2nd ed. 1971), p. 157.
   Note that while Ref. 8 and 9 agree fairly closely, neither author gives an original reference for Nixon.
10. James MacGregor Burns, *Roosevelt - The Lion and the Fox*, (New York: Harcourt, Brace and Wood, 1956), p. 3.
11. *New York Times*, 2 July 1967, p. 1.
12. William Spence Robertson, *Iturbide of Mexico*, (New York: Greenwood Press, 1968), p. 115.
13. Manly P. Hall, "Horoscope of the United States," *Aquarian Agent*, vol. 4. no. 2, May-June 1974.
14. Alan Bullock, *Hitler, A Study in Tyranny*, rev. ed., (New York: Bantam Books, 1961, p. 1.
    [For time conventions see: Max S. Metz, *Ephemeriden 1890-1950*, (Zurich, 1971), p. 414.]

15. Moritz Busch, *Bismarck - Some Secret Pages of His History* (London: MacMillan and Co., 1898), 1: 478.
16. *Encyclopaedia Britannica*, Vol. 10, 1972, p. 325.
17. Lois M. Rodden, *The American Book of Charts*, (San Diego, CA: ACS Publications, Inc., 1980), p. 372.
18. Foreign Broadcast Information Division, Central Intelligence Agency, *Daily Report, Foreign Radio Broadcasts*, Far East No. 190, Far East, Articles and Speeches, 3 Oct 1949, p. 14.
19. *New York Times*, 15 Aug 1947, p. 1.
20. James Bunyan and H.H. Fisher, *The Bolshevik Revolution 1917-1918*, (Stanford: 1934), pp. 109-38.
21. George Lenczowski, *The Middle East in World Affairs*, 4th Ed., (Cornell, 1980), p. 470.
22. *New York Times*, 19 June 1953, p. 1.
23. L. P. Elwell-Sutton and George Lenczowski, eds, *Iran Under the Pahlavis*, (Stanford: Hoover Institution, 1978), p. 27.
24. *Los Angeles Times*, 1 Feb 1979, p. 1.
25. *New York Times*, 15 July 1958, p. 1.
26. Bernard Postal and Henry W. Levy, *And the Hills Shouted for Joy*, (New York: David M. Kay, 1973), p. 179.
27. *New York Times*, 23 Mar 1946, p. 6.
28. *New York Times*, 23 Nov 1943, p. 5.
29. *New York Times*, 2 Sept 1969, p. 1.
30. David Holden and Richard Johns, *The House of Saud*, (New York: Holt, Rinehart and Winston, 1981), p. 96.
31. Ref. 21, p. 326.
32. *Proceedings and Documents of United Nations Monetary and Financial Conference, Bretton Woods, New Hampshire, July 1-22, 1944*, (The Department of State, 1948), 1:1107-16 and 11:1224.
33. John Paxton, "A Dictionary of the European Economic Community," *Facts on File*, (New York, 1977), p. 38.
34. *New York Times*, 28 Dec 1945, p. 1.
35. Faud Rouhani, *A History of OPEC*, (New York: Praeger, 1971), p. 77.
36. *The Times of London*, 26 Mar 1957, p. 8.
37. Stephane Groneff, *Manhattan Project*, (Boston: Little, Brown and Co., 1967), p. 88.
38. Samuel Glasstone, ed., *The Effects of Nuclear Weapons*, rev. ed, (US Atomic Energy Commission: 1962), p. 672.
39. Ref. 38, p. 673.
40. *Scientific American*, (November 1957), p. 66.
41. Ref. 37, p. 385. Note that the information in Ref. 38 is incorrect by one hour for this event, because war time was not properly taken into account.

42. Ref. 38, p. 680.
43. *New York Times*, 26 June 1945, p. 1.
44. *New York Times*, 25 Oct 1945, p. 1.
45. *New York Times*, 8 Sept 1949, p. 1.
I wish to express a special thanks to Larry Ely for providing me with the references from his files, or information that helped lead me to them for the following references: 6, 7, 10, 13, 14, 18, 26 and 43.

Dynamic Astrology Software

Early in 1984, Dynamic Astrology Software for the home computer is planned to be available from the following companies. Information on specific computers, availability, prices and related software can be obtained by writing:

Matrix Software
315 Marion Avenue
Big Rapids, MI 49307

Astro-Graphics Services
217 Rock Harbor Rd.
Orleans, MA 02653

Dynamic Astrology Reports

Astro Computing Services has implemented the predictive techniques described in this book using programs supplied by Dr. Whitney. Various options are available and appear on the Astro Computing Services order form.

To receive an order form and description of all Astro Computing Services reports for astrologers, write to the address shown in the ad on the last page of this book.

INDEX

The best value in everything you need

to calculate and interpret charts

from

ACS Publications, Inc.

P.O. Box 16430, San Diego, CA 92116

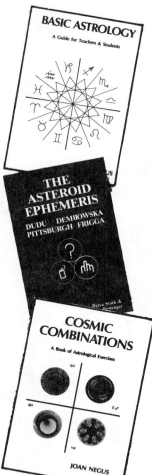